Discard

=== *DYNAMIC MODERN WOMEN* ===

POLITICAL LEADERS

Laurie Lindop

Twenty-First Century Books
A Division of Henry Holt and Company
New York

To Mom and Dad for their love,
support, and encouragement.

∾

Twenty-First Century Books
A Division of Henry Holt and Company, Inc.
115 West 18th Street
New York, NY 10011

Henry Holt® and colophon are trademarks of
Henry Holt and Company, Inc.
Publishers since 1866

Published in Canada by Fitzhenry & Whiteside Ltd.
195 Allstate Parkway, Markham, Ontario L3R 4T8

Library of Congress Cataloging-in-Publication Data
Lindop, Laurie.
Political leaders / Laurie Lindop—1st ed.
p.   cm. (Dynamic modern women)
Includes bibliographical references and index.
Summary: Highlights the lives of ten women prominent
in U.S. politics, including Barbara Jordan, Elizabeth Dole,
Janet Reno, Geraldine Ferraro, and Jeane Kirkpatrick.
1. Women in politics—United States—Biography—Juvenile literature.
2. Women in public life—United States—Biography—Juvenile literature.
|1. Women in politics. 2. Women—Biography.| I. Title. II. Series.
HQ1412.L563   1996
320'.082-dc20   96-11431
|B| CIP
                                                        AC

ISBN 0-8050-4164-8
First Edition—1996

Designed by Kelly Soong

Printed in Mexico
All first editions are printed on acid-free paper.∞
1 3 5 7 9 10 8 6 4 2

Photo credits
p. 6: Gifford/Gamma Liaison; p. 16: Courtesy of the office of Senator Feinstein;
p. 26: Jeff Christensen/Gamma Liaison; p. 36: Franz Jantzen/Collection of the
Supreme Court of the United States; p. 46: AP/Wide World Photos; p. 58: Diana
Walker/Gamma Liaison; p. 68: Courtesy of the Ronald Reagan Library; p. 78:
Cynthia Johnson/Gamma Liaison; p. 88: Paul Howell/Gamma Liaison; p. 100:
Stephen Ferry/Gamma Liaison.

CONTENTS

INTRODUCTION

⊱

This book tells the stories of ten trailblazing contemporary women American political leaders. Many have achieved "firsts"—the first woman mayor of San Francisco, the first African-American congresswoman from a southern state, the first woman vice-presidential candidate.

Some of these women are liberals, others conservatives. Some are married; others are single, divorced, or widowed. Some lived in poverty and faced economic hardships, while others grew up in stately homes. Some of them encountered racism or anti-Semitism. All had to combat sexism and were challenged to prove that women can accomplish as much as men.

As political leaders they have been at the forefront of change and cleared a path for other women to follow in the future. They have guided foreign policy and pushed through groundbreaking domestic legislation; slashed taxes and brought peace to cities ravaged by riots; run massive charitable organizations and helped local townspeople build parks and other needed facilities. Their stories are ones of triumph.

ONE

❧

Elizabeth Dole

When President George Bush would meet with his cabinet members, there would be only one woman seated at the table—Elizabeth Dole, the secretary of labor. Earlier, during Ronald Reagan's presidency, she had been the first woman to become the secretary of transportation.

In 1987 she surprised everyone by leaving politics to become the head of the American Red Cross. Employing her typical competent zeal, she embarked on an ambitious plan to revitalize and modernize one of our nation's oldest and largest charitable organizations.

Her husband is influential Republican Senator Robert Dole, and they have been called one of Washington's top power couples. Senator Dole once joked about his wife's popularity: "South Dakota is noted for Mount Rushmore [the monument on which are carved the faces of four presidents]. Elizabeth was there just last week for a fitting."[1]

❧

Elizabeth, who was called Liddy when she was young, was born on July 29, 1936. She grew up in the small, picturesque town of Salisbury, North Carolina. It was the sort of place where neighbors greeted each other with a friendly nod and a strong handshake, and where people proudly unfurled their American flags on holidays.

Liddy's father, John Hanford, ran a successful flower business. He wanted to provide his daughter with as many advantages as he possibly could, including piano, ballet, and tap-dancing lessons.

Her older brother, Johnny, had been sent to fight overseas in World War II. His parents feared that one day they would get a letter saying that their only son had been killed. "Mother wore a path to the mailbox," Elizabeth said. "Thinking she simply wanted more mail, I wrote home at least once a day [from summer camp]."[2] Everyone rejoiced when Johnny finally returned home.

The Hanford family was very religious, and every Sunday morning they would attend church. Sunday afternoon, Liddy would often go to her grandmother's house to eat cookies and listen to Bible stories. As a young person she developed the vital faith that remains one of the cornerstones of her life.

In high school Liddy was a top-notch student and involved in many extracurricular activities, including the French club, the drama club, and the school newspaper. She loved going to dances, double dating, and having slumber parties. She was always fashionable, wearing poodle skirts and angora sweaters, and even painting the rims of her glasses to match her outfits.

In her senior year she was elected class president and the next semester decided to run for school president. This was considered a boy's job, but her campaign manager pointed out that if Queen Elizabeth could rule Britain, then a girl could be president of Boyden High School. Some of the boys ripped down her posters, and she lost the election. Her mother said, "It didn't seem to bother her. She felt real complimented [that they took her campaign seriously]."[3]

She went on to Duke University, where she majored in political science and said, "I was thinking that law might be a very good background for a career in government service. That was beginning to jell, but it wasn't yet a plan or a blueprint."[4] Her mother hoped that after her daughter graduated she would get married and settle down in a house near her own. But Liddy had other plans.

She decided to take a job in Boston working as a secretary to the head librarian at Harvard Law School library. She spent the next summer at Oxford University in England studying English history and government. As she said, "I had no intention of limiting my education to the classroom. . . . I rode my bicycle out to . . . the Mitre Hotel for tea and crumpets. On weekends I rambled through the Welsh coal-mining valleys."[5]

This trip whetted her wanderlust, and she convinced her parents to let her visit the Soviet Union. "To me, it was one more challenge, a chance to go where few Americans had been."[6] During her trip she spent time with a Russian family who was fearful that their apartment was bugged and kept the radio on the whole time she was there.

When Liddy returned to the United States she enrolled at Harvard and received a master's degree in teaching and government. A few years later she enrolled in Harvard Law School and started calling herself Elizabeth.

Immediately she realized she was entering a predominantly male and often sexist environment. On her first day a male student said, "What are you doing here? Don't you realize that there are *men* who would give their right arm to be in this law school, men who would *use* their legal education?"[7]

Some professors refused to call on the women students. In one case, the only time they were acknowledged was at the end of the year when they were told to get up in front of the class and recite a poem of their own composition!

After graduating Elizabeth decided to move to Washington, D.C., the nerve center of the nation's government. She passed the bar exam, which allowed her to practice law, but felt she wasn't really prepared to do so. She'd never studied trial law and decided to spend a few months learning what she could.

She visited a night court, and the judge, noticing the attractive, young woman in the back of the room, asked her what she was doing there. When she told him, he said, "I have a case for you."[8] He wanted her to defend a man who had been accused of petting and annoying a lion at the National Zoo.

"It's ridiculous to keep a man locked up on a charge like [that]," Elizabeth told a group of reporters. "We're going to trial tonight. Even though I've never seen a trial except on [the television show] *Perry Mason*."[9] She won the case by proving that without the lion as a witness, no one could know for sure if it had actually been teased or annoyed.

Before long Elizabeth was working as a public defender, a lawyer who represents poor citizens accused of crimes. "I was defending alleged drug addicts and armed-robbery suspects. I look back now and marvel at the chances I took prowling around some of Washington's meanest streets looking for witnesses."[10]

In 1968 she took a job working for the White House Office of Consumer Affairs. Anyone who felt cheated by a company or a product could contact this office. Elizabeth read stacks of letters from people complaining about shoddy products, poor workmanship, deceptive packaging, misleading advertisements, and useless warranties.

"What began as just a job soon turned into something of a personal crusade," Elizabeth said.[11] Many of the consumer-protection policies that we take for granted today were started during Elizabeth's tenure.

"We persuaded manufacturers to date supermarket items for their freshness and to identify the source of fats and oils in their products," she said. "Cosmetic firms agreed to list on the label of creams and lotions the full ingredients, including any substances that might cause allergic reactions. A simple philosophy guided us. For consumers to make wise choices, they must have access to all relevant information."[12]

She soon developed a reputation for wanting to know all the facts before she reached a decision. "I am a meticulous person," Elizabeth has said. "And I like to understand the details."[13] Some critics have charged that in all of her jobs, she is too concerned with trying to understand every side of an issue. Nevertheless, her hard work earned her widespread praise, and in 1970 she was named Washington's Outstanding Young Woman of the Year.

Two years later Elizabeth met a handsome senator from Kansas, the Republican Party chairman, Bob Dole. He said later, "It took me several months to work up the nerve to ask Elizabeth out. But it wasn't that long before I saw in her a genuineness and a sensitivity to others that are rare in power-hungry Washington."[14]

While Bob and Elizabeth were getting to know each other, the position of commissioner of the Federal Trade Commission (FTC) opened up, and Elizabeth was offered the job. The FTC is a government agency that probes possible misconduct by large corporations.

Once a vigorous department, the FTC had been gradually losing influence and importance, until it was nicknamed "the Little Old Lady of Pennsylvania Avenue."[15] Elizabeth helped turn the FTC once again into a powerhouse. One of her first actions was to slash 145 of the agency's unnecessary and bureaucratic rules, some of which were designed to regulate industries that didn't even exist any more.

She also began waging war on unethical companies. For example, she brought down one company that was marketing quack cures. Elizabeth also helped revamp the nursing home industry. She made it a priority to help push through Congress the Equal Credit Opportunity Act, which ensured that women had as much access to credit at their banks as men had. Elizabeth Dole wanted citizens to know that she and the FTC were there to fight on their behalf.

Elizabeth knew that things were getting serious with Bob when he started sending her champagne and flowers. "He never got down on his knees, " Elizabeth said. "Come to think of it, I don't even remember a formal proposal. We just gradually began to think of the future as something we wanted to share."[16] In 1975, when she was thirty-nine years old, she married him in a church in Washington, D.C.

Less than a year later Bob was notified that he was Gerald Ford's choice for vice-presidential running mate in the 1976 election. Elizabeth recalled, "*Ford's pick*. The words barely registered. Just enough to send alarms out in all directions. My emotions were definitely mixed. Of course I was proud of Bob and happy about his achievement, but I also felt that a distinct change was about to occur for a couple only recently married. The honeymoon was over."[17] She decided to take a leave of absence from the FTC to campaign with her husband.

That didn't mean, however, she was planning to play the role of the passive political wife. "As an independent career woman, and an FTC commissioner with ten years of government experience, I wasn't going to spend the whole campaign answering reporters' questions with a demure 'I don't do issues.' I did do issues. Six days a week."[18]

On election night, the ticket of Ford and Dole was narrowly defeated by Democrats Jimmy Carter and Walter Mondale. Bob Dole returned to the Senate, and Elizabeth Dole went back to the FTC.

In 1980 Bob decided to run for the Republican Party's nomination for president, and this time Elizabeth resigned from her post to work on her husband's campaign. Bob faced a tough challenge and lost his party's nomination to the popular former governor of California, Ronald Reagan.

Bob later joked, "I pulled out of the 1980 presidential contest at about the same time Elizabeth passed me in the polls."[19] The Doles threw their support behind Reagan, and he won the presidential race in a landslide victory. Elizabeth was then asked to become head of the White House Office of Public Liaison (OPL).

"If the White House were a business," Elizabeth once said, "Public Liaison would be the marketing and sales division."[20] Her department's job was to make certain that the White House stayed in touch with the desires of the American voters and that once official policy had been drafted, it got as much support as possible.

When President Reagan decided to cut the national budget and slash taxes, he relied on the OPL to help build public support. Before these potentially controversial proposals were put to a vote, Capitol Hill was swamped by more than a million messages from citizens voicing their support. Elizabeth Dole and the OPL could take much credit for bringing about this stunning response.

Impressed by her work, President Reagan in 1983 asked Elizabeth Dole to become his secretary of transportation. Her duties were staggering. She worked on such tasks as overseeing the movement of hazardous waste, funneling money to the states for highway repairs, and encouraging businesses to invest in the exploration of outer space. Her department had a $27 million budget and 102,000 employees.

Elizabeth stated that her top priority would be "to promote safety in all forms of transportation."[21] She worked to get drunk drivers off the roads, to push for random drug testing of those responsible for operating transportation equipment, and to fight for improved air quality. With her southern charm and keen political knowledge, she was a successful negotiator.

One staffer admitted, "We were ready for her to fall on her face because we thought it would take a year for her to catch up with everything. But it just hasn't happened. . . . We're trying to keep up with her."[22]

In 1988 Bob Dole once again decided to run for the Republican Party's nomination for president, this time against Vice President George Bush. Once again Elizabeth resigned her job to help her husband campaign. "This is not giving up my career just to sort of stand by his side," Elizabeth assured her supporters. "This is going to be a very active role that I'll be playing in the campaign."[23]

She went on the road with her own press secretaries and strategists, giving speeches in an average of twelve different towns and cities a day. Some suggested that if Bob won, they should run on a Dole-Dole ticket.

"That's a great idea," Bob joked. "But can I be president for at least the first term?"[24]

He lost the nomination to George Bush. For a while some politicians speculated that Bush would pick Elizabeth as his running mate, but he chose Dan Quayle instead. After becoming president, Bush selected her as secretary of labor. She would oversee 18,500 employees and a $31 billion budget.

Elizabeth Dole saw her mission as helping develop policies and programs that would make it easier for people to obtain good jobs. She also worked on issues she felt strongly about: helping women and minorities fight workplace discrimination, and encouraging young people to stay in school.

Soon after being sworn in she found herself in the middle of a battle about the minimum wage (the minimum amount of money an employer must pay workers). For eight years the rate had stayed at $3.35 an hour. The Democrats wanted to raise this rate significantly, but the president proposed a more moderate increase (to $4.25 an hour), which Elizabeth supported and helped push through Congress.

After two hectic years as secretary of labor, Elizabeth was approached by the American Red Cross. The organization was seeking a new leader. Elizabeth Dole was their top choice.

She found the offer very tempting. As the head of such an organization, she would have a chance to help many needy and vulnerable people. With a million American volunteers, the Red Cross is one of the largest charitable organizations. She accepted the job and announced, "I decided that the best way I can let volunteers know their importance is to be one of them."[25] Further, she promised to donate money from her speeches to the Red Cross.

Right away Elizabeth rolled up her sleeves and got to work. She put forth a massive plan to improve the blood services by offering more effective screenings for HIV (the virus that causes AIDS) and other blood-transmitted diseases. When the United States entered the Persian Gulf War in 1991, she headed a massive aid drive and traveled to the Middle East, bringing much needed supplies to the hospitals.

"The part I love," she said, "is that you deal with dire human needs on a full-time basis. It really is a joy to feel that what you're doing is making a difference for someone."[26]

There is speculation that she may, someday, return to public office. One Republican strategist even said, "She's presidential material."[27] In 1996 her husband won the Republican party's nomination for president and Elizabeth once again announced that she would be leaving her job to campaign on his behalf. However, she stated that if Bob were elected, she would not become a "co-president," but would then return to her job at the Red Cross.[28]

"I tell youthful audiences," she said, "they can find no higher calling in life than that of public service. They may not get rich, but they'll enrich the lives of countless others. Along the way, they can raise society's sights and elevate its standards. And when the times comes to look back, as inevitably it will, they can take pride in having been an active part of the struggle of their times. Because of them, the world is a little better."[29]

TWO

DIANNE FEINSTEIN

In 1992 Dianne Feinstein became the first woman senator from California. In 1994 she managed to narrowly win reelection in one of the nation's nastiest campaigns.

Her political career has been a roller-coaster ride of stunning victories as well as a number of heartbreaking defeats. As a moderate, she has often come under fire from liberals as well as conservatives, but she has never given up trying to establish a common ground between them. She has bravely weathered many personal catastrophes, including the death of her husband and the murder of her colleagues. In 1994 she proved she was one of the most resolute politicians on Capitol Hill by almost single-handedly pushing through a ban on assault weapons.

To outsiders, young Dianne's family life seemed picture-perfect. Her father, Leon Goldman, was a respected and wealthy Jewish surgeon. Dianne's mother, Betty Goldman, was a beautiful Russian immigrant. The three Goldman girls—Dianne,

Yvonne, and Lynn—lived with their parents in Presidio Terrace, one of the wealthiest neighborhoods of San Francisco. But inside their lovely home, things were far from perfect.

Betty Goldman suffered from mental illness, which was especially bad when she had been drinking. "We'd be doing our chores," Dianne recalled. "Everything would be fine. . . . And one thing, say we'd drop something, and that would set it off."[1] Betty once apparently tried to drown Dianne's younger sister and another time chased Dianne with a knife. The family treated Betty's illness as something that had to be silently endured. "We lived on tenterhooks," Dianne said, "but you didn't talk about it, because there's nothing you can do."[2]

Dianne attended one of the finest private high schools in the city, Sacred Heart. There, learning refined manners and social graces was as important as learning arithmetic and English. Later, Dianne would often rely on her Sacred Heart etiquette training when meeting with foreign dignitaries or hosting important banquets. Once, when she greeted Queen Elizabeth of England, an impressed commentator said, "It was hard to tell who was more regal."[3]

Dianne thrived at Sacred Heart, receiving A's and B's in her classwork, playing guard on the basketball team, joining the horseback riding club, and serving as the president of the athletic association. She also performed in many of the school's plays. Her sisters recalled how she would stand in front of the mirror rehearsing "every line, every gesture, every expression, every intonation of hands and body."[4]

As a teenager Dianne was introduced by her Uncle Morris to the inside workings of San Francisco's city government. He took her to a Board of Supervisors meeting and she was greatly impressed. "Dianne," he told her, "you get an education and you can do this job."[5]

After graduating from Sacred Heart, Dianne studied political science at Stanford University. In her senior year she helped breathe life back into the school's Young Democrats

Club and became the student body vice president, the highest office a woman could hope to win.

Upon graduating, Dianne went to work for Democratic mayoral candidate George Reilly. "We worked to all hours of the night," Dianne said. "It was the rough and tumble old days of San Francisco politics. I learned how much I loved it."[6]

Although Reilly lost the election, Dianne had no time to be dejected because she had been offered a job studying the city's criminal justice system. It was here that she met her first husband, Jack Berman. He was a brash, thirty-three-year-old prosecutor working for the district attorney's office. Dianne eloped with him to Los Angeles and later gave birth to their daughter, Katherine.

After three years of marriage, they divorced. At the age of twenty-four, Dianne was a single mother living on alimony. A friend recalled how one morning Dianne was "complaining about how early Kathy always woke her up, how she liked to get up to watch the garbage truck. Then the governor called."[7]

Governor Edmund "Pat" Brown offered Dianne a position on the five-member board that set prison terms and parole conditions for women inmates. "I found sitting in judgment of another human being very difficult," Dianne said. "I lost twenty-five pounds the first year on the board."[8]

Shortly after joining the board, Dianne met Bertram Feinstein, a well-respected neurosurgeon. He was nearly twenty years older, but charming and distinguished. Less than a year later Dianne agreed to marry him. "He was the sun, the moon, and the stars," Dianne recalled. "It's fair to say that as a marriage, it was a ten. We just never were apart."[9]

After four years on the parole board Dianne was appointed to the Advisory Committee for Adult Detention, which inspected and reported on the conditions of the jails. The report her committee issued was filled with descriptions of swarming lice and the vile food served to prisoners. The press jumped on the accounts and Dianne made headlines.

With this publicity she decided to take her first dive into elective politics and ran for the Board of Supervisors. She said later, "When I decided to run I knew it was an uphill battle and that the odds were not great. I decided to give it a year and the level best I could. So I started early, went out and asked people to support me, and put together a good little team."[10] That little team, comprised of Bert, her father, and a campaign manager, raised more money than any of her rivals. Dianne also became the first local candidate to use television commercials to her advantage. On election night she came in first, much to the surprise of everyone.

As the top vote getter, she was awarded the board presidency, and she became the first woman to ever hold this position. Riding high on her success, she entered the mayor's race but finished an embarrassing third. She refused to be deterred and began to plan a political comeback. As one friend put it, "No matter what Dianne goes through, she tends to come out stronger. When she gets angry, she can be at her best. When you push her against the wall, she's really terrific!"[11]

In 1973 she was reelected as supervisor and two years later decided to run once again for mayor. She campaigned as a moderate, a candidate who could bring together San Francisco's many groups: gays and straights, whites and minorities, the poor and the wealthy, the elderly and the young. But once again Dianne finished third. "I'm a centrist, basically," she said, "And what happened was, I got squeezed very clearly between the left and the right."[12] The more liberal candidate, George Moscone, won.

The worst news was still to come. On her birthday, June 22, 1976, her beloved husband told her that he had been diagnosed with cancer. Two years later he died. Devastated and emotionally drained, she lost her will to carry on in public life. The morning of November 27, 1978, she told a few reporters that she had decided to quit politics. But by that evening her life and the political life of the city would be turned topsy-turvey.

One of Dianne's colleagues on the Board of Supervisors was a conservative ex-fireman named Dan White. After being elected he found out how difficult it was to support a family on a supervisor's pay. He resigned, but a few days later he changed his mind and asked Mayor Moscone for his job back.

Upon the urging of liberals, including openly gay supervisor Harvey Milk, the mayor turned White down. He figured it would be better to replace White with someone more in line with his own more liberal views.

Dan White was furious and on November 27 stormed into Moscone's office, pulled out a .38 pistol, and shot the mayor five times. White then raced past Dianne's office and into the office of Harvey Milk. Hearing gunshots, Dianne frantically pushed open Milk's office door. He was slumped against it and as she reached for his pulse, her fingers slipped into a bullet hole. Both Moscone and Milk had been murdered.

As soon as the news broke, the city was in shock. People wondered, How could this happen? Dianne Feinstein, as the president of the Board of Supervisors, was next in line for the mayor's office. The woman who only hours before had been ready to end her political career stepped into the glare of the public spotlight and proved to be an effective leader. The *San Francisco Chronicle* stated, "She was poised. She was eloquent. . . . . And she was reassuring and strong."[13]

It seemed as if Mayor Feinstein was everywhere, talking with people, trying to help heal the city. She wanted to make San Francisco a better place to live and nothing escaped her notice. Every Saturday morning she would go out on neighborhood improvement patrols, helping residents paint over graffiti. When she was driving through town, she'd jot down notes about problems she spotted and then would pester state employees until they fixed them.

"I am a perfectionist," she admitted. "And I drive myself hard and the people around me hard, and if it's a problem for anybody, they're welcome to resign."[14]

She hadn't been mayor long when Dan White was put on trial, charged with the murders of the mayor and Harvey Milk. White's lawyer argued that his client had been driven to murder because he was depressed. This depression, the lawyer said, was caused in part by the tremendous amount of junk food White ate. This became known as the Twinkie defense. And it worked! White was sentenced to under eight years in prison, and the city erupted in anger.

San Francisco's gay and lesbian community was especially outraged. Harvey Milk, the first openly gay supervisor, had been murdered and now his killer was getting off with little more than a slap on the wrist. Thousands of angry marchers stormed City Hall.

The police chief ordered his officers not to disperse the mob because he feared this might incite more violence. Dianne supported the chief's decision. Many protesters started hurling rocks, cans, and bottles at the police. The officers, in full riot gear, held their ground. Tensions mounted. Finally the chief gave the police the go-ahead to clear the area. Some frustrated officers began beating the protesters.

Four days later the riots ended. Feinstein found herself being criticized by two groups that had traditionally supported her—the police and the gay community. The mayoral election was drawing near, and Quentin Kopp, a supervisor who had decided to run for mayor against Dianne, attacked her on radio talk shows for allowing the riot to get out of hand.

The race was neck and neck, but Feinstein managed to win. This was due partly to the gays and lesbians who, in the end, decided to throw their support behind her. On December 11, 1979, she became the first woman ever elected to San Francisco's highest office. Twelve days later she married Dick Blum, a tall, athletic, and extraordinarily wealthy investment banker.

As mayor she continued to pursue a moderate agenda, even though it was sometimes unpopular. Nevertheless, by steering a middle course, Feinstein helped to bridge the gulfs between the city's liberals and its conservatives.

In 1984 Walter Mondale, the Democratic Party's nominee for president, considered asking her to became his vice presidential running mate. In the end, he decided to run with Geraldine Ferraro, partly because he was concerned that there would be controversy over Feinstein's husband's financial record. Ironically, the same problem dogged Ferraro.

Blum's money did help finance Dianne's race for governor in 1990. Early on, she was forced to the sidelines while she recovered from an emergency operation. When she returned, her campaign manager quit, telling reporters that Feinstein didn't have "the fire in the belly" to win the nomination. She shot back, "I had a fire in the belly and had it removed."[15]

Her standing in the polls was falling, but then Feinstein released a television ad with a voice-over that boomed, "Forged from tragedy!" It showed dramatic video clips of her bravely taking over the leadership of San Francisco after the Moscone and Milk murders, bringing peace and unity to a devastated, frightened city. She won the Democratic nomination. In the runoff, however, she narrowly lost to the well-funded moderate Republican Pete Wilson.

Dianne bounced back. She spent the next two years putting together a well-financed, well-organized campaign and in 1992 won a Senate seat. She joined a record number of women moving into Congress in what became known as "The Year of the Woman." Many of these female candidates capitalized on voter outrage at a drama that had played out on Capitol Hill a few months earlier.

Americans had sat riveted in front of their television sets watching a Judiciary Committee composed of all-white, all-male senators weigh the testimony of a little-known African-American law professor named Anita Hill. Hill had accused

President George Bush's Supreme Court nominee, Clarence Thomas, of sexual harassment. Hill described how Thomas had made sexual comments to her when he was her boss.

Eventually the senators decided that Hill hadn't presented enough proof to warrant additional hearings. Thomas was sworn in to the highest judicial office in the country.

Feinstein was outraged. She stated, "There is no question that if the Judiciary Committee had women on it, the whole issue [of Thomas's nomination] would not have moved [been settled] until it was explored fully."[16]

After becoming a senator Feinstein vowed to join the Judiciary Committee and quickly became one of its most powerful members. She also single-handedly pushed through a ban on assault weapons, sponsored a desert-protection act, and kept up her strong pro-choice, pro-death-penalty views.

Within two short years Dianne Feinstein was forced to run for reelection because she had taken over a seat that had been vacated early by Pete Wilson when he became governor. The Senate rules stated that she had to run for reelection in 1994 when Wilson's six-year term would have ended. During her short time in office, Dianne Feinstein had put together an impressive record, and normally this would make her an easy winner. But 1994 was not a normal year.

Voters were dissatisfied with politics as usual and an anti-incumbency mood was sweeping the country. Voters in California were especially frustrated by the rising costs of illegal immigration being shouldered by taxpaying citizens. On the ballot was a controversial measure known as Proposition 187, which would deny services to illegal immigrants, including schooling and health care. The initiative was popular with many voters, but analysts questioned its constitutionality.

Feinstein's opponent, a conservative congressman, Michael Huffington, came out in support of the measure, and his standing in the polls rocketed up. Feinstein warned that the initiative could throw many young people out of school and onto the streets. "I know that a majority of Californians support [it] but I will not support Proposition 187. I know that this could cost me votes, possibly even the election."[17]

For a while prospects looked bleak for Feinstein. Huffington had inherited a vast Texas oil fortune estimated at $75 million dollars, and by the end of the campaign, would chip in $28 million of his own money. He blitzed the airwaves with negative commercials that accused Feinstein of coddling criminals and of being a puppet of special-interest groups.

"You can only let yourself be punched for so long before you punch back," Feinstein said.[18] When she punched back, Feinstein punched back hard. She produced TV commercials that portrayed Huffington as an empty suit and that questioned his outspoken wife's involvement with religious cults.

By election night it was clear the race would be tight. Whichever candidate won more absentee votes would represent California in the Senate for the next six years. After Feinstein was declared the winner, she said, "When they told me it was impossible, I became absolutely determined to do it."[19]

The impact of Feinstein's groundbreaking career on the lives of ordinary people is evident in a story she likes to tell. It happened when she was mayor:

"One of the people who supported me said that he had walked into his house one day and his seven children were sitting around the living room play-acting. One of his daughters was in the big chair. He said to her, 'What are you doing in the big chair?'

"She said, 'We're playing mayor and I'm the mayor.'

"The father asked, 'Well, how come *you* are the mayor?'

"And one of the boys answered, 'Everybody knows only a girl can be the mayor.'"[20]

Feinstein grew up at a time when everybody thought that only men—white men—could be mayors and senators. She proved them wrong. And in doing so, she opened the door for others to follow.

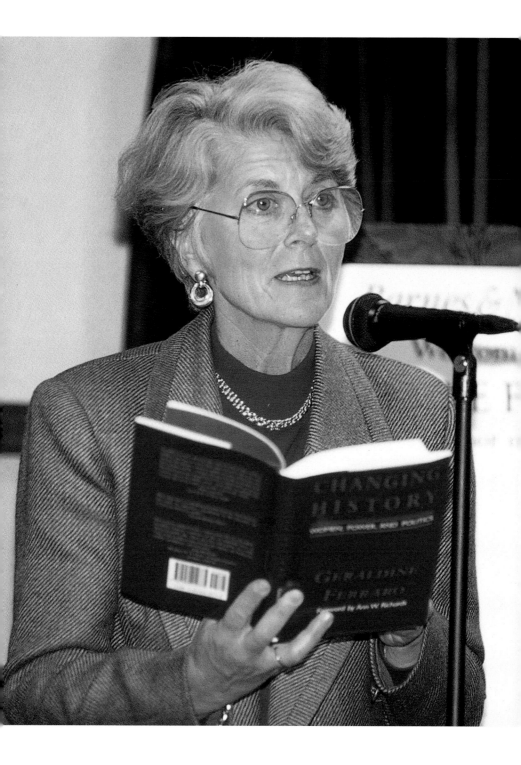

THREE

~

GERALDINE FERRARO

On July 19, 1984, Geraldine Ferraro became the first woman in the history of the United States to accept a major party's nomination for vice president. Standing in front of the cheering crowd at the Democratic Convention in San Francisco, Ferraro said, "As I think of the honor this great convention has bestowed upon me, I recall the words of Dr. Martin Luther King Jr., who made America stronger by making America more free. He said, 'Occasionally in life there are moments which cannot be completely explained by words.'. . . Tonight is such a moment for me. My heart is filled with pride."[1] Everyone there knew that they were witnessing history. Sixty-four years earlier, women had finally won the right to vote. Now a woman was nominated for the second most powerful office in the country.

Ann Richards, later the governor of Texas, said, "I remember thinking not about whether [the Democrats and Ferraro] would win or lose, but thinking about my two daughters. . . . My thoughts were of all the young women across America. They already had won."[2]

When Geraldine Ferraro was born, her parents, Antonetta and Dominick, rejoiced. A few years earlier they had lost their second son, Gerard, in a car accident. They were devastated. But when Geraldine was born, the family was once again full of laughter, fun, and joy.

"We always loved [Geraldine] for herself," Antonetta said. "But we always felt she had the spirit of Gerard within her."[3] Dominick was so delighted he threw a birthday party for his daughter every month of her first year. He converted the restaurant he owned in Newburgh, New York, into a five-and-dime store and would bring his "princess" gifts almost every day.

When Geraldine (Gerry) was eight years old, her father suffered a massive heart attack and died. Since the family had few savings, Antonetta was forced to sell off their possessions to pay for food and clothing. They moved from the suburbs to a small, cheap apartment in the Bronx, a borough of New York City. Despite their lack of money, Antonetta made certain that her children obtained the best possible education. She enrolled Geraldine's older brother, Carl, in military school and arranged a scholarship for Gerry at Marymount, a Catholic boarding school.

Gerry later said, "My mother wanted me to succeed so that I could have more than she could give me. She wanted me to have it all."[4] Gerry didn't disappoint her mother and became a member of the honor society, the French club, the literary society, and the debating club. She also played field hockey, soccer, and other sports.

One of her friends recalled, "Sometimes you meet people and you say to yourself, 'they have great potential.' [Geraldine Ferraro] was one. . . . She was an extremely nice person, but you knew nothing was going to stand in her way."[5]

When she was a senior, Gerry managed to win a partial

scholarship to the expensive Marymount Manhattan College. To help pay for the other half of her tuition, she sold handkerchiefs at a department store. At night she took teacher education courses at Hunter College.

During her junior year she met her future husband, John Zacarro. Although in love, she told him that before they could get married, she wanted to earn a law degree.

Those were hectic years. During the day Gerry earned money teaching second grade at PS 85 in Queens, and at night she attended classes at Fordham University Law School. There was only one other woman in the class of 179 students. A number of her professors and some students felt she was taking a man's rightful place. This just made her want to work harder and she graduated with honors.

Right away John Zacarro gave her a diamond ring and asked her to marry him. With her typical energetic zeal, Gerry took the New York bar exam and got married during the same week. She told her new husband that when she began to practice law, she wanted to keep her maiden name as a tribute to the sacrifices her mother made to further her education.

Gerry soon realized, however, that it would be more difficult than she thought to find work as a lawyer. Despite her excellent academic record, she was told by Wall Street firms, "You're terrific, but we're not hiring any women this year."[6]

For most of the 1960s and 1970s Gerry served as a parttime legal adviser to her husband's successful real estate business. The rest of the time she was busy taking care of their three children. One of her daughters said, "When were little, she was always carting us from lesson to lesson."[7]

When all of her children were school-age, Gerry asked a cousin who was a district attorney for a job. He made her his assistant district attorney in 1974, and in 1975 she moved to the newly created Special Victims Bureau, which handled cases involving abuse of children and the elderly, as well as domestic violence.

"Working with victims of crime," Gerry said, "I saw first hand that there were real limitations to how much the current laws could help people. . . . I wanted to make a difference in the most direct way I could, to create opportunities instead of neglect. It was my neighborhood, and these people were my neighbors, and so in 1978 I ran for Congress in the Ninth District of Queens, New York."[8]

In order to be placed on the ballot, she had to get a minimum of 1,500 signatures on a petition. The week before the deadline, Gerry didn't have nearly enough signatures, so she and John stood outside the shopping center begging people to sign her petition. Moments before the deadline, they raced to the filing office and turned in enough signatures.

Gerry had planned on spending around $25,000 on the election but ended up spending more than ten times that amount. She got this money by selling some real estate she owned and borrowing the rest from her husband and friends. Later, when running for vice president, this became a source of controversy, but at the time, she thought it was perfectly legal.

She won 54 percent of the vote and defeated the Republican candidate, Alfred DelliBovi, a New York assemblyman. She said later, "When I won the election, I knew from the beginning what I wanted for the people of Queens: a congressional office that functioned as a store front, where people could feel free to walk in off the street any time and find someone to help them."[9]

Shortly after entering Congress she was assigned to the House Post Office and Civil Service Committee and used her position to push through changes in local zip codes that resulted in lowering insurance costs of residents back home in Queens. "It was the little nickel-and-dime stuff that over the course of the years added up," one of her campaign advisers said. "It meant a lot to [voters]."[10]

She was loyal to her constituents, but also felt that "it was important for me to vote for what I thought was right, despite political risks."[11] She supported the Equal Rights Amendment, and although she was Catholic, she was a strong advocate of abortion rights.

Gerry also fought hard on behalf of working women. She said, "I felt terribly frustrated by what seemed to be the male indifference [in Congress] to . . . the economic predicament confronting women of all ages."[12] She was outraged to discover that women were making sixty cents for each dollar that men earned. New York City secretaries (mainly women) earned less than parking attendants (mainly men)![13] To address these wrongs, Ferraro, along with her female colleagues, helped draft the Women's Economic Equity Act.

In 1983, after easily being reelected, Gerry was appointed to a seat on the Budget Committee, a panel that sets budget goals for the United States government. She grilled defense experts about wasteful spending. Why, she demanded, did they pay $17.95 for a jet engine bolt that was worth 67¢?

In November 1983 Gerry was invited to dinner by a group of powerful, savvy women politicians, who called themselves "Team A." Team A was convinced that the only possible way the Democratic Party could win the 1984 presidential election was with a woman on the ticket. Ronald Reagan would be running for reelection, and Team A felt that the Democrats could capitalize on voter frustration over the Reagan administration's apparent poor record on women's issues. They told Geraldine Ferraro that if she was interested, they would instantly start pushing her as their top nominee for vice-president.

Gerry was worried about how this would affect her family. Ever since she became a congresswoman, she had lived in a tiny Washington, D.C., apartment that was so cramped her husband didn't like to visit. As a vice presidential candidate, she knew her life would be even more hectic. When she told John about Team A's offer, she warned him that everything about their personal lives would be brought out in public. John nodded thoughtfully and said, "Go for it!"

Support for a female vice presidential candidate was growing. The June 4 cover of *Time* magazine read: "And for Vice President . . . Why Not a Woman?" On July 11 Walter Mondale, the leading Democratic candidate for the presidency, telephoned her and asked if she would be his running mate.

"That would be terrific," Ferraro answered.[14]

Eight days later, at the Democratic National Convention, Ferraro accepted her party's nomination. The crowd burst into cheers. Never before had a woman stepped so close to the most powerful office in the United States.

In her speech that evening, she made a promise. "To all the children of America, I say: The generation before ours kept faith with us, and like them, we will pass on to you a stronger, more just America. Thank you very much."[15]

The Republicans didn't waste any time launching their first attack against Gerry. They announced that she and John had not paid enough income taxes. Immediately Gerry promised to reveal all of their tax returns. This was a mistake.

Husband John had told his wife that in the interests of his business and his personal privacy, he didn't want to do this. Forced to retract the promise, Gerry ended up fueling the rumors. Was she trying to hide something? John finally agreed to release their tax statements to the press.

At first it seemed that they had actually paid more than their share of taxes. But soon the media revealed that on other investments, Gerry and her husband owed back taxes and fines of $53,000. Immediately she sold numerous bonds and paid off this debt. But the damage had been done.

She decided that she had no choice but to hold a press conference and address the public's concerns. She wanted to explain to American voters that she hadn't intentionally avoided paying the taxes, that it had been a mistake. She took a deep breath and walked up to the sea of microphones.

For ninety minutes she answered every question the press asked. She was calm and straightforward. *Time* magazine's headline read, "Under Pressure, Ferraro Passes a Vital Test."[16]

Soon she set out with Mondale on a whirlwind campaign, speaking in little towns and big cities from California to Maine. "No one was ever going to be able to criticize me for not knowing the issues, for not putting the time in, for not trying hard enough. . . ." Gerry had vowed. "No one was ever going to say that under pressure, a woman would fall apart. But it was rough."[17]

Demonstrating her toughness became one of her goals. She knew that, as a woman, she had to prove to voters that if she ever had to assume the presidency, she could successfully take over the president's role as the Commander in Chief of the Armed Forces. She had to prove that, if necessary, she would have the backbone to lead our country into war. "I'm prepared to do whatever is necessary in order to secure this country and make sure that security is maintained. . . ." Gerry asserted.[18] But she also added that it was important for a leader to do everything possible to avoid having to use force.

Gerry also had to defend her stance on abortion rights. The archbishop of New York City, John O'Connor, stated that, "Ferraro had given the impression that . . . you can be a good Catholic and believe in abortion. . . . [But] there is no flexibility, there is no leeway. It is the task of the Church to reaffirm that abortion is death. It is the killing of innocent creatures."[19]

Gerry telephoned the archbishop and told him that she had never "made a public statement . . . [about] the [abortion] teachings of my church."[20] After that a fragile truce existed between them, but abortion rights continued to be a hotbed of controversy throughout the campaign.

Gerry looked forward to publicly debating these important issues with the Republican vice president, George Bush. She said, "I had to prove for all the women of America that I could stand toe-to-toe with the Vice President of the United

States and hold my own. . . . It's not just for me. It's for every one of us to show we're as good as [men]."[21]

She began practicing in mock debates. One of her staffers would play George Bush. They videotaped her performances and dissected her every move. Her coaches gave her endless advice:

"Take the pencil out of your hand."

"Speak s-l-o-w-l-y."

"Look up."

"Stand straight."

"Don't lean on one foot."

"Don't turn your shoulder in."[22]

With practice her answers became clearer and more concise. Finally everything was ready, except for what she would wear. Once again her staffers had many thoughts on the matter, but her daughter Donna showed up with a suit that Gerry loved. It was both businesslike and vice presidential.

The debate went well. Ferraro said, "I took it a question at a time, thankful when each one passed, bringing us closer to the end."[24] At one point Bush tried to lecture her by saying, "Let me help you with the difference, Mrs. Ferraro, between Iran and the embassy in Lebanon . . ." It gave her a chance to prove her mettle. She retorted, "Let me say first of all that I almost resent, Vice President Bush, your patronizing attitude that you have to teach me about foreign policy."[24]

Later, she explained, "No one likes to have her intelligence not only questioned but dismissed, as Bush had done to me. I won't sit still for that under any circumstances. And I certainly wasn't about to in this critical debate."[25]

Afterward Gerry was confident that she had won the debate, but surveys suggested that most Americans felt it had been a draw.

With twenty-four more days until the election, Reagan and Bush were still ahead in the polls. Gerry said, "We pulled out all the stops. . . . As we flew from one time zone into another and then back again, no one could figure out what time it really was."[26] During those whirlwind days, she logged more than 30,000 miles. Everywhere she went, the crowds were huge. Over and over again she roused boisterous cheers when she shouted, "Are we going to win in November? You bet we are!"

But as election day neared, the polls showed Reagan and Bush pulling farther and farther ahead. She said, "I felt so frustrated—and sad."[27] On the night of the election she quietly watched the results coming in. One after the other, states were going for her opponents. One television map showed almost all the states in blue for the Republicans.

She knew it was over. It was time for her to make her concession speech. She stepped in front of the glare of the television lights and said, "For two centuries, candidates have run for President and not one from a major party ever asked a woman to be his running mate—until Walter Mondale. . . . My candidacy has said the days of discrimination are numbered. American women will never be second-class citizens again."[28]

After the election she faced a two-year inquiry into the funding of her congressional campaign, and her son, John Jr., was arrested for the possession and sale of cocaine. "I reeled with disbelief," Ferraro recalled.[29] She blamed herself and her candidacy, but John took full responsibility for his actions. He is now clean and owns a restaurant in Manhattan.

In 1992 Ferraro ran for the U.S. Senate. Once again questions about her husband's financial dealings forced her to go on the defensive. She ended up narrowly losing in the Democratic primary to New York State Attorney General Robert Adams.

Whether or not Ferraro decides to run for office again, her impact on American politics will never be forgotten. Perhaps one day a woman will become vice president or even president. A tough-minded congresswoman from Queens helped pave the way.

FOUR

❧

RUTH
BADER GINSBURG

When Ruth Bader Ginsburg was twenty-seven years old she applied to be a law clerk for a Supreme Court justice. Despite her outstanding academic record, the judge told her, "I don't hire women."[1] Subsequently, Ginsburg dedicated her legal career to fighting this sort of sexual discrimination. On August 10, 1993, thirty-three years after being told she was not eligible to be a clerk for the Supreme Court, she placed her left hand on a Bible and was sworn in as one of its justices.

❧

Ruth Bader was born on March 15, 1933, the descendant of Jewish immigrants from central Europe and Russia. Her older sister, Marilyn, died of a brain disease when Ruth was only a year old.

Ruth's mother, Celia, was the most influential person in her life. A brilliant woman, Celia had longed to go to college but was denied this opportunity because her father felt that higher education would be wasted on a girl. Instead she was sent to work at a garment factory, and her hard-earned wages were used to pay for her brother's college tuition.

When Ruth was born, Celia vowed that her daughter would have the chance to go to college. Every week she stashed away a little bit of the household money, saving up to pay for Ruth's tuition. This was often difficult because America was in the middle of the Great Depression, and although Ruth's father worked seventy hours a week in the clothing industry, wages were very low and he found it hard to make ends meet.

The family lived in a small two-story house in a bustling, crowded neighborhood of Brooklyn, New York. Every afternoon Celia would hustle her daughter out the door and take her to the library. There they would read aloud from the books, breathing in the delicious smells of the Chinese restaurant next door.

During Ruth's childhood Brooklyn was home to people from almost a hundred different nationalities, races, and religions.[2] Sometimes prejudices flared. Early in her life Ruth encountered anti-Semitism: "I have memories as a child," she said, "of being in a car with my parents . . . and there was a sign in front of a restaurant and it said *No Dogs or Jews Allowed.*"[3]

Ruth graduated from elementary school as the top student in her class. In high school she continued to earn excellent grades. One friend said, "[Ruth] never thought she did well on tests but, of course, she always aced them."[4] During Ruth's freshman year Celia was diagnosed with cervical cancer. This intensified the pressure Ruth felt to succeed. She could never forget, not even for a moment, that her mother was counting on her to fulfill her dream of going to college.

As her mother grew sicker Ruth kept her concern to herself, and few of her classmates knew there was anything wrong. She was serious but also outgoing—a member of the pep club called the Go-Getters, a cheerleader, a baton twirler, the editor of the school newspaper, a member of an elite honor society, and a cello player in the school orchestra.

On the night before Ruth's graduation, Celia passed away. She died knowing that Ruth had won a scholarship to Cornell University in Ithaca, New York. Ruth gave the money Celia had saved for her education to her father. "Be independent," Celia had always told her.[5] And Ruth was.

At Cornell Ruth majored in government. In her free time she dated a fun-loving chemistry major named Martin "Marty" Ginsburg. He came from a wealthy Long Island family and enjoyed playing golf more than studying. After graduating from Cornell, he went to Harvard Law School for a year. Ruth graduated with top honors, and soon after they were married. Ruth planned to join Marty at Harvard Law, but he was drafted into the army.

The newlyweds moved to Fort Sill, Oklahoma, where he was stationed. Ruth looked for a job on the army base, but there was little work available for women. She finally found a job as a clerk-typist at the local Social Security office. She became outraged when she discovered that Native Americans were routinely denied their fair share of Social Security benefits because they did not have birth certificates.

"Do you have a fishing license?" she would ask the Native Americans. Usually they did, and this document would contain their birth date. She would then grant them their appropriate benefits.

She had not been working at the office long before she became pregnant with their daughter, Jane Carol. As soon as Ruth's boss realized that she was going to have a baby, he demoted her. At the time this was actually legal. Ruth would store away the memory of this experience and later wage war on laws that discriminated against pregnant workers.

When Marty was discharged from the army, the young parents returned to Boston. Marty continued his studies at

Harvard Law School and Ruth entered the same program. At first she was worried about juggling her studies with taking care of their baby. But they found a baby-sitter, and Marty agreed to do half of the housework—and all of the cooking when Ruth presented him with a warm, grayish, inedible dish that she claimed was tuna casserole!

Ruth's experience of being a student at Harvard was very different from Marty's. She was told that as a woman she was not allowed to enter the old periodicals room in Harvard's Lamont Library, and when the dean invited Ruth and the eight other women in her class to his house, she recalled that he glowered at them and demanded, "Do you realize that you are simply taking the place of a qualified man?"[6]

Ruth set out to prove that she was as good as any of the male students. She was so driven that she became known as "Ruthless Ruthie." By the end of her first year, she was at the top of her class and had made the *Law Review*.

During her second year of law school Ruth found out that once again someone she loved had cancer. This time it was her husband. His prognosis was bad. "We made a decision to take one day at a time," Ruth recalled.[7] Radiation treatments made Marty pale and weak. To help him, Ruth attended all of his classes, took notes, and helped him write his papers. "He got the best grades he had ever gotten," she later joked.[8]

Almost unbelievably, Marty recovered from cancer (though it would take years for them to know that he had been fully cured). When he graduated from Harvard he was offered a job with a law firm in Manhattan. Ruth transferred to Columbia Law School, which is also in New York.

She tied for the highest grades of anyone in her class and earned many other academic honors. If she had been a man, such an achievement would have almost certainly guaranteed her a lucrative job. But she said, "Not a single law firm in the city of New York bid for my employment."[9] She applied to be a law clerk for a number of judges (including Supreme Court

Justice Felix Frankfurter), but they didn't want to hire a woman. She considered teaching law, but was discouraged to find that at that time there was not a single woman faculty member at any major law school. "A woman, a Jew, and a mother," she said. "Three strikes. It was too much."[10]

Finally Ruth found work as a clerk for a federal district judge in New York. Later she spent two years working as a research associate at Columbia. In 1963 she became the second woman ever to join the faculty of the Rutgers University Law School in New Jersey. She was described as a knowledgeable, demanding teacher, though some students complained that she was "a little dull."[11] At the time, Ginsburg was one of only twenty women teaching law in the country and was paid less than male professors.

Two years later, when she became pregnant with their son, James, she remembered the discrimination she had suffered because of her first pregnancy. She was worried that her teaching contract would not be renewed if Rutgers discovered she was having a baby. She started wearing baggier and baggier clothes to hide her expanding girth.

While teaching at Rutgers, Ruth Bader Ginsburg read Simone de Beauvoir's groundbreaking book about sexual discrimination called *The Second Sex*. She found it "staggering."[12] Many women, like Ginsburg, were obtaining a new consciousness about sexism in the 1970s. Across the country women were staging protests against sex discrimination.

During this time Ruth agreed to work as a consul to the American Civil Liberties Union (ACLU), an organization that defends the rights and freedoms of individuals. The ACLU began to refer sex-discrimination cases to Ginsburg because such cases were perceived to be "women's issues"—even if some cases were brought by men!

One of the first cases Ginsburg tried reminded her of her own experience. She defended a group of teachers who had been forced to take unpaid leave because they were pregnant.

Her success fighting for the rights of these women impressed the national director of the ACLU, and she was given her first case to be tried before the Supreme Court.

The Supreme Court is the highest court in America. Eight associate justices and one chief justice serve on the court. They are appointed for life, and when one justice retires or dies, the president nominates a candidate to fill the vacancy. This candidate must be approved by the United States Senate.

The Supreme Court justices review the actions of lower courts and determine whether these actions abide by the provisions of the United States Constitution.

Each year the court receives more than 4,000 requests to review cases but only hears about 150.[13] Ruth Bader Ginsburg brought six cases before the Supreme Court and won five of them.

Her first case, *Reed v. Reed*, challenged the constitutionality of an Idaho law. A boy named Richard Reed had died, and both of his parents petitioned the Idaho court for permission to serve as executor of the boy's estate. The Idaho court awarded the position to the boy's father because the law automatically gave preference to men over women, no matter who was more qualified. Ginsburg proved that this law was discriminatory. The Supreme Court overturned the lower court's ruling and decided in favor of the boy's mother.

This success led the ACLU to found the Women's Rights Project in 1972, with Ginsburg at its helm. That same year she became the first woman to become a tenured (permanent) professor at Columbia Law School.

Ginsburg quickly found that "race discrimination was immediately perceived as evil, odious, and intolerable. But the response I got when I talked about sex-based discrimination was 'What are you talking about? Women are treated ever so much better than men.'. . . Their notion was [that] women were spared the messy, dirty, real world, and they were kept in this clean bright home. And so it was trying [difficult] to educate the judges that [this] . . . was limiting the opportunities, the aspirations of our daughters."[14]

Ginsburg wanted to establish that under the Constitution men and women should always be treated equally. She began trying cases in which *men* had been discriminated against. In doing so, she proved that almost any law that treats men and women differently is unconstitutional. It was an innovative strategy, allowing her to fight sexual discrimination without raising the ire of many who were vocally antifeminist. For example, Ginsburg argued that widowers should receive the same Social Security benefits routinely given to widows. She also argued that husbands should get the same benefits as wives of military personnel.

She based her arguments on the Fourteenth Amendment to the Constitution, which guarantees equal protection of all citizens. The amendment was enacted after the Civil War to protect blacks, but Ginsburg demonstrated that it could also apply to women's rights. Many nicknamed her the Thurgood Marshall (the lawyer who successfully fought *Brown v. Board of Education of Topeka* that brought an end to segregation in schools) of sex-discrimination law.

One of her colleagues stated that Ginsberg's "intellectual force was overwhelming. Her work was very clear, very orderly. She never guessed, she never weaseled, she always was thoroughly prepared. She always knew all the facts and all the law of every case she cited."[15] This sort of preparation and mental ability helped Ginsburg win most of the cases she brought before the Supreme Court. In doing so she almost "single-handedly" forced the court to end sex-based discrimination.[16]

During this time Ruth also was raising a family. Her son said, "A night did not go by when my mother did not check to see that I was doing my schoolwork."[17] To relax, she liked to listen to opera, play golf, go horseback riding, and water-ski.

In 1980 President Jimmy Carter appointed Ruth Bader Ginsburg to serve as a judge on the United States Court of

Appeals for the District of Columbia. (Ms. magazine reported that another female judicial candidate, while waiting to be screened by a Carter-appointed panel, was asked by the chairman to make coffee!)[18] Marty Ginsburg quit his lucrative job with a law firm in New York so he could move with his wife to Washington, D.C. There, he became a professor at Georgetown University.

During the next thirteen years Ruth heard cases involving some of the most controversial issues of our times, including abortion rights, affirmative action, and homosexual rights. Her daughter said, "She's very struck by what happens to people. She would say to me, 'We're not only talking about grand abstract principles, we're talking about *people.*'"[19] Ginsburg insisted on taking her law clerks to the prisons and hospitals where inmates would be sent to make certain they realized how a court's ruling impacted on the lives of real people.

As a judge Ginsburg was cautious and respectful of legal precedent. One court expert stated, "Ruth stopped being an advocate when she went on the court."[20] Nevertheless, her rulings revealed her underlying support of individual rights, free speech, and freedom of religion.

This judicial restraint appealed to President Bill Clinton. In 1993 Justice Byron White announced his retirement from the Supreme Court. For the first time in more than a quarter of a century a Democratic president had the chance to appoint a justice to the court. For eighty-seven days Clinton pondered whom he would pick. He wanted someone "who when the name is heard people say, 'Yes. Wow. A home run.'"[21]

His staff put together a list of fifty possible choices. The president narrowed it down to three. He met with each of the candidates. He was very impressed by Ginsburg. He later said, "Once I talked with her, I felt very strongly about her."[22] He also stated that she "cannot be called a liberal or a conservative. She has proved herself too thoughtful for such labels."[23]

An example of this involved Ginsburg's stance on abortion

rights. At first the media seized on her criticism of the *Roe v. Wade* case, which legalized abortion. She thought the case had been argued from a tactically questionable angle and suggested what she thought would have been a better, different strategy. Eventually people realized that although she didn't like *Roe v. Wade*, she was firmly supportive of a woman's right to choose abortion.

Some conservatives, like Senator William Cohen of Maine, worried that she was "a political activist who's been hiding in the restrictive robes of an appellate judge."[24] But most senators and many members of the press praised Clinton's choice. One reporter gushed, "In Ruth Bader Ginsburg [the president] has chosen a justice who has the potential to bring everlasting honor to his name."[25] Bob Dole, Senate Republican leader, said she was someone who "undoubtedly has the experience and intellect to hit the ground running if confirmed."[26]

Ginsburg had to win approval from the Senate Judiciary Committee before she could be confirmed. From July 20 to 23, 1993, she met with the senators and fielded their questions. She declined to predict how she would vote on issues that might come before her as a justice, but she did state that the courts should lead on social issues "when political avenues become dead-end streets."[27]

She was easily confirmed by a vote of ninety-six in favor to three against. On August 10, 1993, Ruth Bader Ginsburg became the second woman Supreme Court justice (Sandra Day O'Connor had been appointed to the Court in 1981) and the first Jew in twenty-four years.

"I pray," Ginsburg said after her nomination, "that I may be all that [my mother] would have been, had she lived in an age when women could aspire and achieve, and daughters are cherished as much as sons."[28]

FIVE

꿈

BARBARA JORDAN

"I get from the soil and spirit of Texas," Barbara Jordan once said, "the feeling that I, as an individual, can accomplish whatever I want to, and that there are no limits, that you can just keep going, just keep soaring."[1] Barbara Jordan's accomplishments serve as testament to this belief. Growing up in poverty, she became the first black woman elected to the Texas state senate and later, the first black woman from a southern state to be elected to the United States Congress.

꿈

Born on February 21, 1936, Barbara Jordan was the youngest of three daughters. Her family's house in Houston, Texas, was so small Barbara had to share a foldout bed with her sisters in the dining room. "We were poor, but so was everyone around," Barbara recalled. "We didn't notice it."[2]

On the weekends she would help her Grandpa Patten collect trash for his junk business. Her sisters thought this was nasty. "They weren't going to put on old clothes and get down into the horse manure sorting old rags and paper and getting dirty," Barbara recalled.[3] But her grandpa had taught Barbara to be as independent minded as himself. "You don't have to be like those others," he would tell her. "You just trot your own horse."[4]

Every Sunday morning Barbara went with her family to the Good Hope Missionary Baptist Church. Her father was an extremely religious man and a strict disciplinarian. He forbade his daughters to go to the movies, to go out dancing, or to read anything but the Bible and schoolbooks. Nevertheless, Barbara managed to have fun with her many friends and especially enjoyed going to football games, where she would cheer louder than the cheerleaders.

She attended Phillis Wheatley High School, which was named for an African-born former slave who was the first black poet to be published. At first Barbara didn't take her education seriously. She said, "I was a person engaged in serious play. And then my mother, father, and sisters said, 'You're never going to amount to anything unless you go to school. You've got to get something in your head.' I decided right then that I sure did want to amount to something, so I went to school."[5]

At that time schools were still segregated—black children went to one school and white children to another. This struck Barbara as wrong. "I did not think it right for blacks to be in one place and whites in another place and never shall the two meet. . . . And it wasn't only the school system, it was everywhere. The church, the city. We would ride on the back of the bus and there was a sign on the bus with a little colored bar, and you had to walk back there to sit."[6] Barbara put forth an argument why this type of segregation should end when she was on the debate team in high school.

At the age of sixteen she showed great promise as a public speaker and in 1952 won an all-expenses-paid trip to Chicago to take part in a national debate contest. She outshone all of the other competitors. Years later she would be named the "best living orator" by the International Platform Association.

After graduating from high school, Barbara went to the all-black Texas Southern University. By then she had already decided that one day she would become a lawyer.

She was especially excited about joining TSU's debate team. The coach took the debaters to tournaments all over the country in his fancy yellow Mercury. However, he told Barbara that he couldn't take her along because, as the only woman on the team, she would need a chaperone. Barbara refused to miss out on the opportunity and methodically began to change her appearance. Instead of wearing fashionable scoop neck shirts and costume jewelry, she started wearing drab blazers and flat shoes. She also gained weight.

The coach decided that she no longer looked like the sort of woman who would need a chaperone and let her join the male debaters on the road. They won almost every tournament they competed in. They even tied the top-ranked Harvard University team.

Driving through the South, the debaters continually encountered the outrages of segregation; they couldn't stay in hotels, go into restaurants, and often found that there were no rest rooms for black people, only outhouses. But when they headed up north, things were different.

"We didn't eat in any fancy restaurants," the coach recalled. "We didn't have that kind of money to spend. But we could at least go in front doors to get something to eat. That was the main point: We could go in the front door."[7]

In 1954 things began to change in the South. A landmark case was brought before the Supreme Court: *Brown v. Board of Education of Topeka*. The Court struck down segregation in public schools as unconstitutional. Barbara was ecstatic. She hoped that at last black children could get the same level of education as white students.

When she left TSU Barbara headed to Boston University Law School. She was one of two blacks and one of five women in the freshman class. The other 592 students were white males. She soon realized that "the best training available in an all-black university was not equal to the best training one developed as a white university student. . . . I was doing sixteen years of remedial work in thinking."[8]

Every day she would sit in the library, hunched over her books, reading, studying, thinking. It would get later and later. Everyone else would go to bed, but Barbara would keep at it. Still, she felt hopelessly behind. After taking her first-year exams, she returned home, dejected. It was a distinct possibility that she had flunked out. She anxiously waited for her grades to arrive in the mail.

When the grades finally did come, she opened the envelope with trembling hands. She had passed! After that first year, law school became easier. When she graduated she managed to pass both the Massachusetts and Texas bar exams (which lawyers must do in order to practice law in a particular state).

At first she thought she would stay in Boston because "the air is freer. . . . I won't have all the hang-ups of segregation."[9] But then she changed her mind and decided that in her heart she was a Texan. To the delight of her parents, she moved back home and set up an office in their dining room.

At this time John Kennedy was campaigning for president. Lyndon Johnson was his vice presidential running mate. Barbara wanted to help them get elected. The local campaign staff sent her out on speaking engagements. "By the time the Kennedy-Johnson campaign ended successfully," Barbara recalled, "I had really been bitten by the political bug."[10]

In 1962 she decided to run for the Texas House of Representatives. She made inspiring speeches that were met with thundering applause and often brought listeners to their feet. On election night she was certain that she would beat her opponent, a white lawyer named Willis Whatley. As the ballots were counted, however, it became clear that although she had strong support from African-Americans, not enough white people had voted for her. She received 46,000 votes but Whatley had 65,000. Jordan tried running for the same seat two years later, and although she won a few thousand more votes, she still lost the election.

Why are you doing this? she asked herself.[11] In her heart she knew why: politics had become the most important thing in her life. She would find a way to win an election.

In 1965 she decided to run again, this time for state senator. The Supreme Court had recently ordered Texas to redesign its voting districts to ensure that blacks and other minorities had nearly equal representation. For Barbara Jordan this meant that she would be running in a newly created district that was 38 percent African-American.

Her opponent in the Democratic primary was Charles Whitfield, a white man who had already served in the senate for two terms. He stated that blacks should not vote as a block for Barbara Jordan simply because she was also black.

Barbara fired back, "Look, don't tell us about black block votes. You know white folks have been block-voting for the past century. We don't have to apologize. Our time has come!"[12]

It had. She pulled off a stunning victory. No Republican wanted to run against her in the general election. So, on January 10, 1967, she became the first African-American to be elected to the Texas legislature in eighty-four years.

She spent her first few months in office learning everything she could about the inner workings of the Texas government. She said, "You work and you learn the rules and you keep your mouth shut until it is time to open it."[13] When she did step into the spotlight, it was in Washington, D.C.

Lyndon Johnson had become president after Kennedy was assassinated. He had pushed through Congress the Civil

Rights Act of 1964, which guaranteed that blacks had many of the same rights as whites. Next he wanted to talk with civil rights leaders about proposed fair-housing legislation, and he asked Barbara Jordan, the new African-American senator from his home state, to present her ideas. After meeting with the president, the *Washington Post* reported, "The White House was far more impressed with [Barbara Jordan] than the usual run of civil rights leaders."[14]

When she returned home Barbara Jordan began to push through legislation that would bring about social change, including a bill that sought to end workplace discrimination. She fought for Texas's first minimum wage law and helped bring about a raise in workman's compensation (which provides benefits to workers injured on the job).

By the end of her first year she was voted Outstanding Freshman Senator. She thanked her colleagues by telling them, "When I first got here we approached one another with suspicion, fear and apprehension, but now I can call each one of you singularly friend."[15]

In 1968 Barbara was reelected to a four-year term. She worked on committees that addressed various problems from environmental matters to youth affairs. On March 28, 1972, she was voted president pro tem of the Texas legislature, making her the first African-American woman to head a legislative body.

As her term neared its end, she began to set her sights on winning a congressional seat. She got some help from President Lyndon Johnson, who described her as "a woman of keen intellect and unusual legislative ability, a symbol proving that We Can Overcome. Wherever she goes she is going to be at the top."[16]

When it became clear that she was going to win the 1972 election and become the first African-American congresswoman from any southern state, her friends in the Texas legislature wanted to honor her before she left for Capitol Hill.

They decided to make her governor for the day. This was a purely symbolic appointment, but one of immense historical importance. Barbara Jordan became the first black woman to serve as governor of any state—even if it was only for a single day.

Her friends and family crowded into the senate chamber to witness her swearing in as governor. Barbara Jordan recalled, "I did not have to tell them to be quiet, because I was the governor, and I could run my day the way I wanted to. So they yelled at everything."[17]

As a freshman congresswoman, she knew that one way she could have a significant impact on government was by serving on an important committee. But which one? She asked her friend Lyndon Johnson for help. He had stepped down from the presidency in 1969 but was more than happy to offer advice. He suggested that she serve on the Judiciary Committee and then pulled some strings to help her get this coveted appointment.

When Barbara Jordan arrived in Washington, the city was already abuzz with rumors about Watergate. In June 1972 five men had been arrested trying to break into the Democratic National Headquarters, which was located in a complex of buildings called Watergate. President Richard Nixon, a Republican, was running for reelection and the burglars were trying to help his campaign by discovering secret information in the Democratic headquarters. As the Watergate story unfolded, questions were raised about whether Nixon knew about the burglary before it took place and, even more important, how much he had been involved in the desperate effort to cover up the scandal. If the president had any serious involvement with these illegal activities, there might be grounds for impeachment (removal from office).

By the time Barbara Jordan was sworn into Congress, in 1973, the evidence against Nixon was strong enough to warrant the formation of a Senate committee to investigate the charges. The committee learned from a presidential aide that Nixon had tape-recorded his White House conversations. The committee ordered the president to turn over the tapes. At first Nixon refused to do this, but when he was finally forced to hand some of them over, a large section of one tape was blank—portions of the president's conversation had been erased.

It was a scandal like none before. Americans were riveted to their television sets, watching with horror as the investigation proceeded. The House Judiciary Committee was assigned to decide whether or not impeachment hearings should take place.

Day after day Barbara Jordan and the other Judiciary Committee members pored over the facts, listened to testimony from key Watergate players, deliberating what should be done. "The big major issue the committee had to deal with was how to define the charge [against Nixon]," Barbara Jordan stated. "The Constitution said that the President shall be removed from office on impeachment for treason, bribery, or other high crimes and misdemeanors."[18] If the committee was going to push for impeachment hearings, it would have to show that Nixon had committed high crimes or misdemeanors. Was there enough evidence to show that there was a reasonable chance he had been guilty of this?

Jordan studied everything she could find that had ever been written relating to impeachment and the Constitution. She wanted to make sure she didn't rush to judgment. It was too important. No president in the history of the United States had been convicted on impeachment charges. She wanted to make sure she did the right thing. After days of deliberation she decided that impeachment hearings were warranted.

The Judiciary Committee decided to hold a televised press conference, during which each member would speak to the American public for up to fifteen minutes. For many viewers, this was the first time they had ever heard directly from the Texas congresswoman.

Enunciating each word, Barbara Jordan stated with both sadness and conviction, "My faith in the Constitution is whole, it is complete, it is total. I am not going to sit here and be an idle spectator to the diminution [lessening], the subversion, the destruction of the Constitution."[19] There was overwhelming evidence, she explained, that the president's actions had violated the Constitution. One CBS news correspondent called her "the best mind on the committee."[20]

After her speech Jordan went off with a group of other legislators into a back room to cry. It was a sad night for all of America.

The House Judiciary Committee voted twenty-seven to eleven to recommend impeachment of the president on the grounds that he had obstructed justice by taking part in the Watergate cover-up. A short time later Nixon resigned. His vice president, Gerald Ford, was sworn in as president.

Soon after this Barbara Jordan received a telephone call telling her that Ford wanted her to join a group of influential legislators on a trip to China. She couldn't pass up such an opportunity and flew halfway around the world. While she was gone she got a telephone call from a reporter asking her, "What do you think of Ford's pardon of Richard Nixon?"

"What?" Barbara Jordan shouted, unable to believe the news that Nixon could not be charged with any crime in court because Ford had pardoned him.

Now, she realized, the American public might never have a chance to really know exactly what Nixon's involvement had been in the Watergate scandal. "The country," she said, "definitely got short-changed."[21]

In 1976 Jordan was asked to join Senator John Glenn, a former astronaut, as one of the keynote speakers at the Democratic National Convention. The Democrats could sense victory in the upcoming presidential election. Delegates were exuberant, dancing through the aisles, shouting and laughing, shaking hands, making jokes. They were certain their candidate, Jimmy Carter, could defeat Gerald Ford.

When John Glenn stepped up to the podium and began to make his speech, many rowdy delegates kept talking and milling around. Watching in the wings, Barbara Jordan was nervous. How would she get their attention? She decided she would just have to trust in the speaking skills she had been developing over a lifetime.

When it was her turn she went up to the platform, squared her shoulders, and began. Her booming, resonant voice filled the auditorium. "If God is a woman," one listener recalled, "she must sound like that."[22]

The delegates turned to look at her as the room fell silent. They were entranced.

"There is something different about tonight," Barbara Jordan told them. "There is something special about tonight. What is different? What is special? I, Barbara Jordan, am a keynote speaker."[23] For the first time, she told them, a black woman was giving the keynote address at a national party's convention.

By the end of her speech, the applause was deafening.

Barbara Jordan returned to Congress, ran for her third term, and was easily elected. As a congresswoman, Jordan fought for civil and women's rights and pushed through legislation that would help the nation's poor. Trying to bring about an end to the Vietnam War, she supported a bill that would prohibit the Defense Department from siphoning money from other programs to support the war. She also fought against the development of the Alaskan oil pipeline, claiming that it would have a harmful impact on the environment.

At the end of her third term Jordan shocked people by announcing her retirement from politics. She said that it had become too "all-consuming."[24] Almost instantly she was given many job offers. She decided to become a full professor at the Lyndon B. Johnson School of Public Affairs at the University of Texas.

"The idea of playing a definitive role in educating young people to go into government was very attractive to me," she said.[25] Her classes were so popular that students were selected by lottery. She had a much-loved tradition of hosting a year-end barbecue for her students and serenading them with anything from "Amazing Grace" to "Money Honey."[26]

She used a wheelchair to move around because, as she put it, "My legs don't work like other people's because of multiple sclerosis. . . . I discovered that my physical impairment did not diminish my thinking or the quality of my mind. And it did not impact on my capacity to talk."[27]

On August 8, 1994, President Bill Clinton awarded Barbara Jordan the Medal of Freedom. It is the highest honor given to a civilian.

"Sometimes," Barbara Jordan said, "I just stare in the mirror and look at myself and I say: 'Barbara, by golly, you done okay. It wasn't easy but you've done okay.'"[28]

On January 17, 1996, she passed away from viral pneumonia at the age of 59. On the cold drizzly morning of her funeral service more than 1,500 people filled the Good Hope Missionary Baptist Church in Houston, Texas, and hundreds more gathered outside to listen to the service on loudspeakers. Both President Clinton and former Texas Governor Ann Richards recalled her powerful presence and lasting legacy that she left upon the country. Actress Cicely Tyson said of Barbara Jordan, "If I were sitting on a porch across from God, I would thank Him for sending you to us."[29] Many in the audience began crying when her debate coach from Texas Southern University said simply, "Barbara, Barbara, Barbara, we thank you for just being Barbara."[30]

SIX

JEANE KIRKPATRICK

On February 4, 1981, Jeane Kirkpatrick was sworn in as the permanent United States ambassador to the United Nations. She is the first woman to hold this post. A patriotic and staunch defender of our nation, she said, "There is only one reason, one, that I am doing this work. . . . I think it's my duty. I have a demanding conception of citizenship. I have an obligation to confront serious problems."[1]

Born on November 19, 1926, Jeane Jordan grew up in the small town of Duncan, Oklahoma—a dusty, rough-and-tumble sort of place. The Ku Klux Klan would charge through the streets terrorizing African-Americans, and oil prospectors would plum the reddish earth hoping to hit a rich vein. Jeane's father, Welcher Jordan, was one of these oil drillers and, like many men in this financially risky business, experienced his fair share of ups and downs. Jeane's mother did the bookkeeping for her husband and took care of Jeane and her younger brother, Jerry. A bright woman, she loved reading and made books seem wonderful and magical to Jeane. In fact, when Jeane was ten, the one thing she wanted more than anything else in the world was a thesaurus!

During her fifth-grade year Jeane's father told the family they were heading north to Vandalia, Illinois, a town that was experiencing an oil boom. At the time Jeane was learning about the Civil War in school from the South's point of view, but when she got to Illinois, it was from the North's. She said later this helped her realize that "the truth is not always self-evident. One side was right, one wrong, and one had to study history to decide [for oneself] which was which."[2]

Two years later the family moved to Mount Vernon, Illinois. Jeane quickly adapted to life in her new school. She had a steady boyfriend, acted in the school plays, edited the newspaper, and earned top grades. She also discovered Shakespeare. "I bought myself the complete works of Shakespeare," she recalled. "I read most of them. The histories and tragedies especially—but I kept this a secret because this was not part of life for a normal girl and I wanted to lead a normal life."[3]

Upon graduating from high school, Jeane attended Stephens College, a two-year all-women's college in Columbia, Missouri. Her father hoped that when she finished she would return to Mount Vernon, marry, and live near them. But Jeane desperately wanted to learn more.

She moved to New York City upon graduating from Stephens and enrolled at Barnard College in 1946. At first she couldn't decide which subject to major in, but finally settled on political science. World War II had just come to an end, and some of Jeane's professors were refugees from war-ravaged Europe. They made the atrocities of Nazism come alive for her. She said later, "It would have been hard to have grown up in . . . [this time] and not develop an acute political consciousness."[4]

At Barnard she also became fluent in French. She would spend hours practicing her pronunciation with her best friend, a native French speaker. Jeane recalled how her friend "heaped scorn on me when I spoke, as she would put it, 'as though I had a mouthful of mashed potatoes,' but she was very patient. She would go over and over the French sounds with me until I got them right."[5]

A dedicated student, Jeane set her sights on becoming a political science professor. After graduating from Barnard she enrolled as a graduate student at Columbia University in New York City. Two years later she had earned her master's degree and had almost finished all of her doctoral work when her father told her he was tired of paying for her education and wanted her to get a job. Devastated, she realized she would have to postpone her dream of a Ph.D.

With letters of recommendation from her professors, she headed to Washington, D.C., and found work with the State Department's Bureau of Intelligence and Research. She analyzed interviews with refugees from the Soviet Union. These people described their escapes from death camps that had been set up by the Communist leader, Joseph Stalin, to punish dissidents. "They were terrible stories,"[6] Jeane said, and they helped make her a strong, lifelong anti-Communist.

The director of her department was Evron "Kirk" Kirkpatrick. Fifteen years her senior, he shared Jeane's passionate love of politics. Now and then he would take her to lunch, and they enjoyed chatting about world events.

After a year in Washington Jeane won a fellowship from the French government. It would pay for her to study at the renowned Institute de Science Politique in Paris where she could continue to work on her doctoral studies. Toward the end of her stay Kirk came to Paris on business and invited her to dinner. They took the same ship back to the United States and for five days ate every meal together. "Except for breakfast," Kirk laughed.[7] Jeane was not a morning person.

Back in the United States they continued to date more seriously, and Jeane found work at George Washington University in Washington, D.C. Once again she interviewed refugees, but this time the people had escaped from Communist China. Their hair-raising stories reinforced her already strong anti-Communist beliefs.

In 1955 she decided to marry Kirk. True to their interest in all things political, they had a wonderful time spending their honeymoon at a political science convention!

A year later she quit work when she gave birth to the first of their three sons, and for the next decade most of her time was devoted to raising the boys. In 1962, when all of her children were school-age, Jeane took a part-time job as an assistant professor of political science at a small women's college, Trinity University. Five years later she became an associate professor of political science at prestigious Georgetown University.

"She's a damn good teacher," one colleague said. "She has a grasp of the fitness of things."[8] While at Georgetown Jeane finished her doctoral work, and at the age of forty-one was finally awarded her long-awaited Ph.D in political science.

By the mid-seventies, the Kirkpatricks were becoming more and more frustrated by the Democratic Party. Although they had been lifelong, active members, they felt that recently their party had drifted too far from traditional Democratic values and was becoming representative of the counterculture. In response, they helped found the Coalition for a Democratic Majority, which combined a moderate view of social issues with a hard-line, anti-Communist stance on foreign policies.

During this time Jeane wrote a book, *Political Woman*. In it she highlighted the absence of women in power, stating that in 1974 there was "no woman in the cabinet, no woman in the Senate, no woman serving as governor of a major state, no woman mayor of a major city, no woman in the top leadership of either major party."[9]

This book and her other writings impressed the members of the American Enterprise Institute (AEI). AEI is one of the nation's premiere conservative political "think tanks"—an organization that sponsors scholars to study a particular topic. They asked Jeane to become their first female senior scholar.

Two years later she published an article in *Commentary* magazine that would influence the course of her life in unexpected ways. It was a strongly worded piece criticizing President Jimmy Carter's foreign policy. She stated that its failure was "clear to everyone except its architects."[10]

Republican presidential candidate Ronald Reagan read her article and realized that her vigorous anti-Communist views reflected his own. He asked her to serve as his foreign-policy specialist during his 1980 campaign against Carter. She said on the television program 60 *Minutes*, "I thought maybe [Reagan] was a right-wing extremist, frankly, but I discovered very quickly that he's no kind of extremist at all."[11] She agreed to help him, and shortly after Reagan won the presidential election, Jeane got a telephone call from him while she was on vacation. "I asked how he was," she recalled, "and he said, 'I'll be better if you agree to be our ambassador to the United Nations.'"[12]

Founded in San Francisco in 1945, the United Nations (UN) was established to settle disputes between nations and "to save succeeding generations from the scourge of war." At first there were only 51 member nations; by the 1980s there were 157 member nations. Its headquarters were in New York City. As an ambassador, Jeane Kirkpatrick knew she would be responsible for representing the United States and our nation's foreign policy at all UN meetings.

It would be a tremendous challenge. She had no practical foreign policy experience and no diplomatic training. She would have to leave Washington, D.C., and her beloved world of writing and research. But she said, "I take the duties of citizenship seriously. And I believe that if one is called upon to spend a reasonable period of one's life in public service in a democracy, that one has an obligation to do so."[13]

In 1981 she took her seat at the horseshoe shaped table of the United Nations. She knew the frustrations of the work were so intense that her recent predecessors had remained at the UN for no more than two years. She would have the added burden of being a woman in a role traditionally held by men. As one observer explained, "Men have dominated [the UN] from the day it was born. By and large, women in diplomacy are not especially popular."[14] Right away Jeane Kirkpatrick found this to be true. Many of her colleagues insisted on referring to her as "Mrs." rather than as "Dr." or "Ambassador."

Nevertheless, she quickly became known for her eloquence. Her sentences were grammatically perfect, and she had a deep voice that she used effectively. One reporter commented, "Theater people have to train for years to get the kind of suspense and thrust Kirkpatrick can get out of an ordinary English sentence."[15] Her critics complained that she sometimes came across as "confrontational" and "schoolmarmish."[16]

From the start she made clear that there were certain things that she was not going to tolerate. One of them was the bashing of the United States. When a group of Third World countries published a statement criticizing the United States' policies toward Libya, Cuba, and the Palestine Liberation Organization, Kirkpatrick felt that these countries were treating the United States as a nation to be "ignored, deplored, despised, and reviled."[17]

The United States had adopted a long-standing unwritten policy of not responding to such attacks. Kirkpatrick declared that this would stop. "I will not suffer in silence when the good name and record of the United States are assaulted."[18]

She fired off sixty-six letters to the authors of the statement, demanding that they explain their support of "such vicious lies."[19] Many felt "The letter was shock tactics and certainly unconventional. . . . [But] It made them [the delegates] sit up and take notice."[20]

Soon, Kirkpatrick began sending Congress the UN voting records of these countries. This helped pave the way for a requirement that a country's UN voting record be taken into account before it was granted financial aid by the United States.

One of the issues Kirkpatrick found difficult to resolve arose shortly after she joined the UN. Israel had bombed a nuclear reactor in Iraq. Israelis claimed it was a necessary action to prevent Iraq from building nuclear weapons that it could then use against them. Kirkpatrick was sympathetic to Israel. But the State Department had issued a statement denouncing Israel that made it unthinkable for the U.S. ambassador to do anything but agree. Further, Israel's action was technically in conflict with the principles of the UN's peacekeeping mission.

She decided she had no choice but to set to work negotiating a compromise that would be as fair to Israel as possible. The resulting resolution was widely praised and Reagan called her a "heroine."[21] Still, Kirkpatrick did not feel good about having to vote to condemn Israel and barely raised her hand. Stepping away from the table, she said, "I feel sick."[22]

As the UN ambassador, Kirkpatrick was also a member of the president's cabinet and attended meetings of the National Security Council (the group of advisers responsible for dictating foreign policy). One White House insider stated, "[The president] listens carefully to her. He knows that she gives stable, serious advice."[23]

She was perhaps most influential in helping guide the administration's response to a difficult situation in Nicaragua. In 1979 that Latin American country had erupted in civil war as citizens rallied against the oppressive regime of President Anastasio Somoza Debayle. At first the United States supported the rebels, known as Sandinistas. Forcing Somoza to flee, the Sandinistas took over the government.

Soon they confiscated large amounts of land that had once been held by Somoza and his friends, and they began to acquire a number of the country's industries. When they restricted the freedom of the press, some Americans worried that the Sandinistas were turning into a Communist regime.

Kirkpatrick supported the Reagan administration's controversial decision to begin funding a group of Nicaraguan rebels known as the Contras, some of whom were once members of Somoza's national guard. In 1982 Kirkpatrick testified before a Senate subcommittee investigating human rights in Nicaragua. She stated that the Sandinistas were restricting freedom of the press and those who criticized the government were punished. She added that the Sandinistas had postponed elections and that they had "moved against labor as well as business, fiercely attacking Nicaragua's independent trade union movement."[24]

A year later the president asked her to visit the country and assess the administration's policy. She returned strongly convinced that the United States should send even more funds to the Contras. The American public, however, was far more skeptical, and Congress refused to increase aid.

In 1984 the press reported that Nicaraguan harbors had been secretly mined by the U.S. government. Many Americans were outraged. It seemed that their government had begun waging a secret war without the consent of Congress or the public. Kirkpatrick maintained that no one had ever discussed this military operation with her and she condemned it. Congress voted to stop all aid and arms shipments to the Contras.

Two years later newspaper reports revealed that even after the funding was cut off, the Reagan administration had continued to send aid to the Contras. Top National Security Council officials were accused of selling arms to Iran and diverting part of the profits to help the Nicaraguan rebels. Kirkpatrick was never implicated in what became known as the Iran–Contra scandal. She defended the administration, suggesting that it had been forced to take extreme measures when Congress cut off aid and therefore interfered with the president's authority to guide foreign policy.

In 1984 she spoke at the Republican National Convention and outlined the philosophy of the administration's foreign policy and her own strongly held conviction: "Our strength, for which we make many sacrifices, is essential to the independence and freedom of our allies and our friends."[25]

By the end of that year Kirkpatrick felt it was time to retire and return to a quieter and more peaceful academic life. The UN, she had found, was a place that encouraged "conflict."[26] She had been working almost around the clock. Every day, she said, "Around eight forty-five it was off to work, and from then on I worked right through the nightly dinner party until I went to bed at one A.M."[27]

Also, she wanted to spend more time with Kirk. She said, "The pain of knowing he was home eating dinner alone was one of the biggest reasons for me to leave the UN." And there was her cat. "Kirk doesn't like cats, and there he was home with my cat!"[28]

When she announced her departure, friends and colleagues were deeply saddened. For two months, night after night, there were parties held in her honor. Even those who had disagreed with her had been impressed by her intelligence, her drive, and the strength of her convictions.

After leaving office, she officially became a Republican. She also continued to advise heads of state about foreign policy. She went back to work at the American Enterprise Institute and wrote frequent newspaper articles.

At the end of her book *Political Women*, Kirkpatrick wrote: "The existence of |political| women . . . in this |book| should encourage those who come after by proving that it can be done."[29] Jeane Kirkpatrick paved the way for Madelaine Albright, the UN ambassador under President Bill Clinton. And she paved the way for any other woman who should ever seek the job.

SEVEN

⤬

Peggy Noonan

Peggy Noonan, the first woman to serve prominently as a presidential speechwriter, authored many of the most eloquent and colorful speeches delivered by Ronald Reagan, the president known as "The Great Communicator." She also crafted some of the best-known phrases of George Bush's presidential election campaign of 1988, including his call for a "kinder, gentler nation."

Irreverent, funny, and a brilliant magician with words, Noonan has said, "A speech is poetry: cadence, rhythm, imagery, sweep! A speech reminds us that words, like children, have the power to make dance the dullest beanbag of a heart."[1]

⤬

"Nothing really memorable happened in my childhood," Peggy has said, "yet I think about it all the time."[2] Born on September 7, 1950, she was the third of seven children in a boisterous Irish Catholic family.

Her father sold appliances and furniture for a large department store in Massapequa, Long Island. Although he worked hard, the wages were low and he barely made enough money to support such a large family. Sometimes Peggy would come home to a dark apartment because the electricity had been shut off; at other times it was the telephone.

With six siblings, Peggy discovered she could grab center stage if she communicated effectively. Sitting at the dinner table, she would quietly plot out what she wanted to say. "I would map out the narrative, sharpen the details, add color, plan momentum. . . . This way I became a writer."[3]

Growing up in a staunchly Democratic family, Peggy fell in love with the Kennedys. "They were Irish Catholic just like us," she recalled. "And they were smart and glamorous with their tuxedos and silk dresses, and they always said the right thing and had a wonderful humor."[4] She even formed a John F. Kennedy Fan Club out in the chicken coop. She would regale her captive, feathered audience with speeches about the wonderful, handsome, young president and the Kennedy clan.

When Peggy was in high school the family moved to an apartment over a candy store in Rutherford, New Jersey. She was not a particularly good student in high school. She described herself as "the class cut up and classic under-achiever."[5] In her senior year she had an eerie dream about the death of Martin Luther King Jr. before he was shot. A little while later she had another odd dream. This time she kept hearing the words "forty-four days," repeating over and over. Forty-four days later Robert Kennedy was assassinated!

After graduating from high school Peggy took what she described as a "soul-deadening" job as a clerk for a life insurance company in New Jersey. At night she attended classes at Fairleigh Dickinson University. After two years she was accepted as a full-time student. For the first time she applied herself to her studies of English literature and journalism and earned excellent grades. She also edited the school newspaper and became politically active.

At this time America was engaged in the Vietnam War. At

Fairleigh Dickinson as well as many other colleges, students were protesting the war. "I was part of the whole scene," Peggy said. "I had long blond hair and aviator glasses and bell bottom jeans and a tight-fitting shirt that had flowers on it."[6]

In 1971 she climbed aboard a bus packed with other war protesters heading for a demonstration in Washington, D.C. She said, "I couldn't get in the spirit, into the swing. . . . There was contempt for the nineteen-year-old boys who were carrying guns in the war. . . . There was contempt for America."[7]

That afternoon Peggy realized that she was not like the protesters. Her own philosophy was more in line with that of the Republican conservatives who she said felt that "America is essentially good, [that] the war is being fought for serious and valid reasons, [that] the answer to every social ill is not necessarily a social program . . . and God is as real as a rock."[8] So Peggy switched parties and became a Republican.

Upon graduating from college Peggy took a job writing news reports for CBS radio in Boston. A year later she was promoted to editorial director. She said that the most valuable lesson she learned during this time was that "when you work on deadline, you can't procrastinate or have writer's block. It doesn't matter if you can't do it—you do it anyway."[9]

In 1977 she was offered a job as a writer-editor for CBS radio in New York City. It was an exciting time to be working in radio journalism and CBS was the heavyweight in the industry. Most of the reporters and writers were men. Women were just beginning to break into journalism.

In 1981 Peggy Noonan became the writer for Dan Rather's radio-commentary show. They rarely agreed on issues, but he respected her intelligence and writing talents. He said he'd make a deal with her: "I'll tell you my view [on a topic]. If you disagree, you've got five minutes to change my mind. If you succeed, we do it your way. If you don't, you'll still get to give a fair presentation of your side, but we do it my way. Ultimately it's going to reflect my views. Because it's my show."[10]

For three years Dan Rather and Peggy Noonan stuck to this deal. But as time passed she began to acknowledge that she didn't enjoy being an objective journalist. She was deeply, passionately partisan. President Ronald Reagan was her hero.

"I yearned," she said, "to help the president, whose views I shared. I ached to write his words."[11] Although she had no connections in Washington, D.C., she vowed to become his speechwriter. She began spreading the word and pursuing connections at CBS. Eventually the head of the Reagan speechwriting department asked her to come to Washington for a meeting and soon afterward offered her a job.

Peggy Noonan left CBS exactly three years after she had started working with Dan Rather. She was thirty-three years old, embarking on her third job after college. This seemed like a good sign.

Her new office was in a building next to the White House. It was tiny and ugly. The radiator clanked. The desk was old, her chair broken, the bookcase stained. But she was thrilled. She was part of the Reagan presidency. Immediately she began to study the great speeches of former presidents. "In time," she said, "I knew I was looking for the grammar of the presidency, the sound and tone and tense of it."[12]

Speechwriting involved much more than just finding the right words, the right tone. Once Peggy had been assigned a speech, researchers would start compiling whatever background material they could find, including an analysis of the president's position on the subject. She would usually have a week or two to work on a big speech, a few days for a smaller speech. When she finished her first draft, up to as many as fifty of the president's advisers would review the speech carefully. They would cut out what they did not like and add other ideas they thought should be included. "This [was] where my heart was plucked from my breast," Peggy recalled, "and dragged along . . . hauled along every pebble and pothole."[13] After incorporating as many changes as necessary, she would send the speech to the president for his comments. She would then go back for the final rewrite.

Shortly after she began working at the White House, Peggy was asked to write a speech for Nancy Reagan, the first lady. She felt she had been picked because she was the only woman speechwriter on the staff. Furious, she threatened to resign unless she was allowed to do what she'd been hired to do—write for the president. It was her first and last speech for Nancy Reagan.

Not long after this incident, Peggy Noonan once again found that she was being treated differently because she was a woman. She had been assigned to write her first big speech commemorating the fortieth anniversary of D day. She said, "I felt like I had to prove to the boss that a girl could do this speech, so I was nervous."[14]

Her speech was an emotional stunner. Turning to the veterans of the war, Reagan read her lovely words: "These are the boys of Pointe du Hoc. These are the men who took the cliffs."[15] After this widely praised speech, the White House began to realize that the young, blond speechwriter had an uncommon talent for crafting powerful sentences, for pulling an audience's heartstrings and stirring its imagination.

But as one observer noted, "It would be a disservice to her seriousness to see Noonan as merely a clever and gifted ghostwriter. In the Reagan administration, words make policy."[16] Noonan echoed this sentiment, stating, "Government is words. Thoughts are reduced to paper for speeches, which become policy."[17]

When, in one of her speeches for Reagan, Noonan referred to the Contras (the Nicaraguan rebels trying to overthrow the Sandinista government) as "the moral equal of our Founding Fathers,"[18] her words were helping to shape and shade the administration's policy toward the conflict. Such words made it abundantly clear that Reagan felt the Contras' fight was just and morally right.

73

Noonan has explained the impact a speechwriter can have on policy by using an example from a speech former President John F. Kennedy gave in Berlin: "If an American president goes to Berlin . . . it is one thing (and one kind of policy) if he says, 'The American people support the German people.' "It's quite another if he says, 'I am a Berliner.' The first means, 'We support you,' the second means, 'We really mean it, we're really here, and if we ever abandon you it will forever be a stain on our honor.'"[19]

In 1984 Reagan ran for reelection and Noonan wrote the stump speech he gave two or three times a day in cities across the country. Some critics claimed the speech was too filled with bighearted optimism and contained few concrete facts about the president's plans for the future. But the speech connected with the mood of the voters, who wanted to feel good about America. Reagan won in a landslide.

During Reagan's second term, Noonan found the president's aides especially difficult to work with. She said, "They were always ejecting elegant words from my speeches because they thought the 'common man' . . . wouldn't understand."[20]

One of the worst editorial criticisms she ever received was for a speech she wrote after the space shuttle *Challenger* exploded, killing the seven-member crew. It concluded with the lines: "We will never forget them, nor the last time we saw them—this morning, as they prepared for their journey, and waved good-bye, and slipped the surly bonds of earth to touch the face of God."[21] When she sent the speech to the National Security Council staffers to read, one of them suggested that she change the last line to "reach out and touch someone—touch the face of God." Peggy took a deep breath and patiently explained that she wasn't going to use a phrase from a telephone commercial![22]

She was much less patient when the staff tried to dilute her fiery, conservative language. One such speech was to be given to the European Parliament in Strasbourg, France, on the fortieth anniversary of V-E Day. It included a blistering attack on the Soviet Union, which Noonan described as the "principal destabilizing influence in the world today."[23] One reporter noted that the speech, "would have let Reagan be Reagan and turn loose his true feelings about the Evil Empire [the Soviet Union]."[24] But the staffers, concerned about how such inflammatory language would affect U.S.–Soviet relations, chopped out most of Noonan's strident paragraphs, rewrote much of the middle, and mellowed the overall tone.

"I was supposed to cave [to their demands]. . . . And I didn't cave,"[25] Noonan recalled bitterly. She fired off an angry memo declaring that the speech in its rewritten form would become known as "the famous Strasbourg Hammock Speech of 1985. The speech . . . in the middle [of which] there was this nice soft section where we all fell asleep."[26]

Later she said, "One of the things I heard after the battle was 'She's a little high-strung, isn't she?' They *might* have said that about a man who is a writer who believes in something and puts it down on paper. They *might* have, but I doubt it."[27]

The director of communications, Patrick Buchanan, felt that Noonan's strongly held hard-line beliefs made her a good writer. He said, "Moderates are never any good as speechwriters. . . . They don't believe deeply, they don't have the passion and intensity."[28]

Noonan's intensity and wit captivated Richard Rahn, the chief economist for the United States Chamber of Commerce. A dashing man, with an eye patch and dark good looks, he asked Peggy to marry him in 1985.

Peggy wanted to become the head of speechwriting at the White House. When this position became available she was advised to make a peace offering to the staffers with whom she'd battled so many times—"tell them you can work with them."[29] But this was not something the independent-minded, fiery writer could do, and she was not given the job. Soon afterward she resigned.

Two years later Peggy was driving to the market with her toddler son, Will, and her mother. They were listening to a radio report about how George Bush's 1988 election campaign for the presidency was foundering. (Bush had been Reagan's vice president. Since Reagan was retiring from the White House, Peggy wanted Bush to win.)

"I turned to my mother," Peggy recalled, "and I said, 'Mom, could you take care of the baby?'" When her mother agreed, she headed off to help the campaign.[30]

"It was the dream of every speechwriter," she admitted, "to come in at a crucial time and make a difference."[31] And this was exactly what she did. She wrote speeches that helped Bush win his party's nomination and then set to work drafting his acceptance speech for the Republican National Convention. It was an important speech. One staffer said, "He'll live by it or he'll die by it."[32]

On the night of the convention Bush told the hushed crowd, "We are a nation of communities of thousands and tens of thousands of ethnic, religious, social, business, labor union, neighborhood, regional and other organizations, all of them varied, voluntary, and unique. This is America. . . . A brilliant diversity spread like stars, like a thousand points of light in a broad and peaceful sky."[33] Many called this the best speech Bush ever gave, and it helped propel him to victory. Noonan said, "I felt as if I'd pulled together the strings of the highest, strongest kites, tied them together, and handed it off to a man who used it to lift him up high."[34]

Although she was offered a job as the president's speechwriter, Noonan turned it down. "I was afraid," she said, "I would become stale and repeat myself."[35] But she did write Bush's inaugural address and Reagan's final farewell.

As the new administration got under way, Noonan separated from her husband and moved to New York. There she wrote her first book, *What I Saw at the Revolution: A Political Life in*

the Reagan Era. It was a candid, often humorous look at life behind the scenes of the Reagan White House.

The public liked the book, and it jumped onto the best-
seller lists. But some, like this former colleague, derided her
for being too self promoting: "Whenever she wrote a good
line, she got up and held a press conference."[36] Others accused her of using "her privileged access as a speechwriter to
take . . . a sneering attitude toward her staff colleagues."[37]

In 1992 Noonan received a call from one of George Bush's
advisers. "We have a disaster on our hands," he admitted.
"The president wants you to come down."[38] Bush was running
for reelection but his prospects looked bleak. Remembering
how Noonan had helped jump-start his candidacy four years
earlier, he was hoping she could work her magic again. She
agreed to help Bush write his State of the Union Address.

Shortly after finishing the speech and meeting with the
president and his staff, she sensed that there was not much
else she could do to help. She sent the president a letter jok-
ingly saying, "I'm more trouble than I'm worth."[39] Bush then
accepted her decision to retire from speechwriting.

Since then Noonan has written another book, *Life, Liberty
and the Pursuit of Happiness*, as well as magazine articles. Also,
she hosted a series on PBS called *On Values: Talking With Peggy
Noonan*. A reviewer said, "Noonan is a good listener. . . . She is
the one who frames and guides these worthwhile chats about
religious faith, families and freedom, while making no attempt to hide her own robust point of view."[40]

Some speculate that she may return to speechwriting in
the future, but she's said that this is not something she wants
to do: "I feel that as much as I love rhetoric [using language
effectively], as much as I think about it, I would rather walk
around with my socks on fire than write a speech."[41]

Kurt Schmoke
Mayor

Janet Reno
U.S. Attorney General

EIGHT

꧁

JANET
RENO

On Friday, March 12, 1993, Janet Reno strode into the Roosevelt Room of the White House to be sworn in as the seventy-eighth attorney general of the United States of America and the first woman to hold this position.

A tall woman—six-foot-two—with a simple blunt hairstyle and oversize glasses, she became one of the most respected officials in the Clinton administration. As our country's top law enforcement official, she won praise for being a tough, hard-driving crime fighter as well as a compassionate advocate for the rights of children, minorities, and women. She declared, "I will set an example that will enable people to understand, if a woman can be attorney general of the United States, she can do anything."[1]

꧁

Janet Reno was born on July 21, 1938, in Miami, Florida. Her parents, Henry and Jane Reno, were dynamic, intelligent people. Henry, a Danish immigrant, worked as a police reporter for the *Miami Herald*, a beat he covered for more than forty years. He kept a desk at police headquarters so that he could be closer to the action and would often bring donuts for the police and his homegrown flowers for the secretaries.

Janet's mother, Jane Wood Reno, also worked as a newspaper reporter and often joked that she had succeeded as a writer despite having failed her journalism course in college. Outspoken and strong willed, she wrestled alligators and trapped skunks; she recited poetry and raised peacocks.

In 1949 Jane decided to build a house on the twenty-one-acre plot of land the family had bought on the edge of the swampy Everglades. "She dug the foundation with her own hands, with a pick and shovel," Janet Reno later recalled. "She laid the brick, she put in the plumbing and my father would help her with heavy work at night."[2] Watching her mother work, Janet learned that it was possible for a woman to do anything she wanted, so long as she set her mind to it. Forty-three years later, the house survived the terribly destructive Hurricane Andrew without losing more than a few shingles.

In addition to Janet, her three siblings, and her parents, the property was filled with a variety of animals, including pelicans, beagles, raccoons, pigs, ponies, and skunks. Janet's sister Maggy said, "Daddy would come out of the bathroom and say, 'Would somebody get this'—and you can interject pelican, otter, boa constrictor—'so I can take a bath.'"[3]

The children loved the outdoors. They would canoe up the still, murky river and swim in waters shaded by the palmettos and gumbo-limbo trees. As a girl, Janet wanted to be a baseball pitcher, a doctor, a marine biologist, and then finally a lawyer, because she "didn't want anyone telling me what to do."[4]

In high school she was an excellent student and lettered in softball and basketball. One of her favorite activities was competing with the debate club. Her mother said it made sense because Janet "can give you a few thousand words—a few thousand well-chosen words—on just about anything."[5]

Janet Reno went to Cornell University in Ithaca, New York, where she majored in chemistry and was president of the Women's Student Government. By her senior year she knew she wanted to become a lawyer and was accepted at Harvard University Law School. Harvard had only started admitting women to their program in 1950, and in 1960 Janet was one of only sixteen women in a class of five hundred students.

At law school she faced a number of instances of sexual discrimination. For example, one professor announced that "he wouldn't call on women in the big classrooms." He said that "their voices weren't powerful enough to be heard."[6] During her second year of law school, Janet applied for a summer job with a Miami law firm. Despite her talent, she was turned down because the firm refused to accept any female lawyers.

Janet worked hard and obtained her law degree in June 1963. Shortly afterward she moved back to Miami and took a full-time job with a law firm. Four years later she became a junior partner in the firm of Lewis and Reno.

In 1971 Janet entered the world of politics as the director of the Judiciary Committee of the Florida House of Representatives. Within a few months, she came up with an impressive proposal to completely reorganize the court system. In 1972 she ran for a seat in the state legislature. She said that the best advice she ever got about campaigning came from a friend who told her, "Just keep on doing and saying what you believe to be right. Don't pussyfoot, don't talk out of both sides of your mouth just to be popular."[7]

Day after day, she tirelessly walked the voters' neighborhoods, going door-to-door with a broad smile and a clear message. Although she lost, she didn't have much time to feel discouraged. The day after the election, Richard Gerstein, the Dade County state attorney, offered her a job organizing a juvenile department for young people who had been arrested. Gerstein's assistant later said, "I figured [Reno] would dawdle around like everybody else and write another report. Instead, she pasted the juvenile court together in about two months."[8]

Her success made such an impression on Gerstein that when he resigned from his post, he suggested that Janet Reno take his place. In 1978 she became the first female state attorney in the history of Florida.

The state attorney is a lawyer (also known as a prosecutor) who represents the state in court cases against people accused of crimes. Janet Reno was in charge of nine hundred employees and responsible for administering a budget of almost $30 million. On the day of her swearing in, she said, "My number one goal is to make the streets safe, and I pledge every effort for the prosecution for crimes of violence."[9]

This, she knew, was not going to be an easy task. Miami was a city ravaged by drug dealing, violence, organized crime, and illegal immigration. She knew it would take all of her talent and a lot of hard work to bring about positive change.

To keep track of her hectic schedule, she recorded all meetings and all important information in a little black book. When employees promised her that they would check up on something or deliver a report to her, Reno would note it in the black book. If they failed to carry out their promise, she would demand an explanation. One of her assistants, Dick Gregorie, laughed, "If she gets you in the book, watch out. When the book comes out you've gotta have an answer."[10]

Eventually Reno became one of Dade County's most popular government officials. But her first few months in office were filled with turmoil, including a race riot.

In the early morning of December 17, 1979, Arthur Mc-Duffie, a black insurance salesman, was speeding on his motorcycle. A policeman spotted him and began a high-speed chase. Eventually he was joined by other white policemen, who caught McDuffie and began beating him with their fists and nightsticks. Five days later, he died in the hospital. Despite eyewitness accounts of the incident, the officers tried to pretend that McDuffie had been hurt in a motorcycle crash.

Reno's office was in charge of prosecuting the policemen. It seemed obvious that the men were guilty, but her attorneys failed to convince the all-white jury of this and the policemen were pronounced not guilty. As the news spread, rioting began to break out in the chiefly black neighborhood of Liberty City.

Some people accused Reno of purposely mishandling the case because she was a racist. She watched as rioters filled the streets, angrily chanting, "Reno! Reno! Reno!" She was deeply hurt by these accusations. "I felt I had always had a strong commitment to civil rights," she said. And she added that if it had been up to her, she would have declared the officers guilty, but verdicts were not decided by her, but by a jury.[11]

For four days Miami was at the mercy of the angry mobs. The sky grew dark with smoke from torched cars and burning buildings. Crowds of people surrounded the justice building, where Reno and other government officials hid inside. When it was all over, sixteen people were dead and there was $200 million in property damage.

Reno said later, "I don't recall the emotion so much as just thinking that I must put one foot in front of the other."[12] She began by organizing prosecutors to charge those involved in the riots. The courts were busy seven days a week, staffed by judges and lawyers working almost around the clock.

Then she began to try to rebuild bridges with the African-American community. Day after day she went into the black neighborhoods to talk with people, to explain that her prosecutors had done everything possible. She offered to meet her critics anywhere, anytime, and was seen standing on street corners late at night, talking with local residents.

Slowly people began to realize that she was sincere. H. T. Smith, a well-known African-American lawyer in Miami, said, "I have gone from being one of her strongest and most outspoken critics to a strong supporter."[13] Five years after the riots, Reno marched in the Martin Luther King Jr. parade through those same streets and was greeted by wild cheers. She was re-elected as state attorney four times. In her last election she was so popular nobody wanted to run against her.

During these years she established herself as a strong fighter for children's and women's rights. She aggressively prosecuted child-abuse and spouse-abuse cases. She went after "deadbeat dads"—fathers who refused to pay child support.

Reno's reputation spread beyond Miami. Shortly after Bill Clinton was elected president, she received a telephone call from members of his transition team. They were trying to put together a list of potential nominees for the job of attorney general. At the time, Janet's mother was very ill and dying of lung cancer. Janet told them that she was too busy nursing her to leave Miami. Her mother died on December 21, 1992.

On February 11, 1993, Clinton nominated Janet Reno as attorney general. During her confirmation hearings in the Senate, the nation watched as this tall, iron-willed woman stepped into the national spotlight and didn't blink. She told the Senate how her mother had built her house and then added, "as I come down the driveway through the woods at night, with a problem, with an obstacle to overcome, that house is a symbol to me that you can do anything you really want if it's the right thing to do and you put your mind to it."[14]

When the hearings concluded, Reno was approved by a vote of 98 to 0. Senator Carol Moseley-Braun praised Clinton for choosing Reno. She said that his decision to pick a woman attorney general sent a strong message to the American public about the talent of women working in the law. She predicted that Reno's appointment would revitalize and bring much needed change to the Justice Department. "[Reno] does bring a perspective that's new: cooperation, coordination," Moseley-Braun stated. "A feminist perspective."[15]

Staffers in the Justice Department quickly found out that

their new boss was accessible in ways that other attorneys general hadn't been. For example, on her first visit to the employee cafeteria, Reno insisted on paying for her lunch even though the cashier offered it to her for free, and she ignored the special table that had been set up for her with a reserved sign and a linen tablecloth. She sat with the rest of the staffers at the Formica-topped tables.

One young lawyer said that this was especially remarkable because "in the past, the attorney general would sit at a private table studded with security agents and you couldn't get within four feet."[16]

Reno explained her philosophy this way: "One of the things I tried to do as state attorney was to be accessible, not to be remote, not to close my door. I think it's important that people feel that the attorney general can be accessible to them so that she knows what's happening on the streets of America and not just what's happening in the hall of the Department of Justice."[17]

Reno had little time to get used to her new job. A series of crises faced her, including an investigation into terrorist bombings of New York City's World Trade Center; probings into possible ethics violations by the FBI director, William Sessions; and a deadly standoff between law enforcement and Branch Davidians, a religious cult in Waco, Texas.

On February 28, 1993, the Bureau of Alcohol, Tobacco, and Firearms (ATF) had bungled an attempt to search the cult's compound for illegal assault weapons. A shoot-out occurred, during which four ATF agents and six cultists were killed. The remaining cult members, including women and children, hunkered down inside the squat buildings of the compound, refusing to surrender. Agents began waging psychological warfare by blasting annoying music at them day and night, aiming bright spotlights through the buildings' windows to disrupt their sleep, and broadcasting appeals from members' relatives. But the cultists refused to budge.

Janet Reno received information that the children inside were at risk of being physically abused by the cult's leader. She felt that something had to be done to rescue them.

On April 19 she made the controversial decision to order tear gas to be pumped into the building. The FBI had assured her that it was nontoxic and would force the cultists to come outside. But the attack did not go as planned. Rather than surrender, cult members apparently began setting fire to the compound. Reno and the nation watched horrified as televised reports showed plumes of dark smoke curling up from the buildings. Eighty-six people, including seventeen children, ended up dying in the fire.

While the ashes still smoldered, Reno walked up to the lectern in the Justice Department and began answering reporters' angry questions. Visibly shaken, she squared her shoulders and took full responsibility for the decision to move in on the Branch Davidians. "I approved the plan," she said. "I'm responsible for it. I advised the president, but I did not advise him as to the details. I made the decision. I'm accountable, the buck stops with me."[18]

Some criticized her for authorizing the bungled attack. But others saw her readiness to accept responsibility as refreshing and heroic—especially since top government officials often passed blame to others.

"She's a powerhouse and she's doing a great job," said Clinton aide George Stephanopoulus. "She speaks with great moral authority."[19]

In the following months, however, Reno's insistence on doing what is right rather than what is politically popular ended up occasionally bringing her into conflict with the Clinton administration. For example, she ruffled some White House feathers by supporting the federal independent counsel law, which would establish an independent lawyer to investigate any wrongdoing by top administration officials. Reno insisted "I have tried to address every question in the

Department of Justice with one overriding issue. What is the right thing to do? Not what is the popular thing to do, but what is the right thing to do."[20]

Reno also continued to bring this message to the public: Families and communities must be strengthened to break the cycle of violence and despair. She wanted to find ways to help young people grow up to be upstanding, law-abiding citizens. She pushed what she called a national agenda for children, which included programs that would provide medical and educational aid to toddlers, reduce teenage pregnancy, and intervene in abusive or neglectful families.

Janet Reno never had children of her own, but her life is filled with young people. Every few weeks she spends time at the Raymond Elementary School, talking with students, sharing books. She also became the legal guardian of fifteen-year-old twins when their parents, friends of hers, died. Her friend Sara Smith said, "Janet would have loved to have a relationship with a man and have children, but she's a very smart woman, and it was difficult to find a man who had both a sophisticated city mind and was an outdoor person—and was not threatened by a successful woman."[21]

Reno once told a group of elementary school students, "When I was your age, they said ladies didn't become lawyers. Ladies certainly didn't become attorneys general."[22] She proved them wrong. She became one of the most popular leaders in American government to storm the capital in years.

She knows she is not perfect and has said, "I do have a temper. I am not a good housekeeper. My fifth-grade teacher said I was bossy. My family thinks I'm opinionated and sometimes arrogant."[23] But she is also determined, intelligent, and approachable. Her honesty is unquestioned, her strength of character almost legendary.

No matter what obstacles she has had to face, Janet Reno always remembers her mother's motto: *Good, better, best. Don't ever rest, until good is better and better is best.*

NINE

❧

ANN
RICHARDS

When Ann Richards opens her mouth, you never know what's going to come out. She's a wisecracking, straight-shooting mother of four, who in 1990 became the first woman elected in her own right to be governor of the state of Texas. This feat was especially remarkable considering that Texas is a state known for its macho, male-dominated politics.

With grit, determination, and humor, she not only overcame alcoholism but also weathered a divorce and came out swinging in a difficult campaign. She set out to prove, "If you give [women] a chance, we can perform. After all, [the dancer] Ginger Rogers did everything that [her partner] Fred Astaire did. She just did it backwards and in high heels."[1]

❧

Ann Richards is fond of saying that her daddy came from a town called Bugtussle and her mama was raised in a place called Hogjaw. Ann grew up in a dusty two-store town near Waco, Texas, called Lakeview. But as she put it, "I don't know why in the world it would be called Lakeview; there was no lake to view."[2]

Her parents were poor but hardworking. Her father drove a delivery truck and her mother grew all of the food they ate, took care of the house, and sewed all of their clothes. Ann recalled how she used to wear "dresses made out of feed sacks, and in the really old days they said Bewley Mills on them, which was a big flour mill. Everything came in sacks—flour, sugar, feed—so we'd get fed and get a wardrobe at the same time."[3]

Born in 1933, she was her parents' only child. They encouraged her to "do whatever you wanta do . . . just get up and go after it."[4] Ann took this to heart. "When Superwoman comics came out I really believed that I could be her," she recalled. "I got on the roof of the garage with a rope—a magic lariat—and jumped off. "[5] Later in life, she would try to be a modern version of Superwoman—a wife, a mother, and a career woman—and would always be plagued by the nagging doubt that she wasn't living up to people's expectations.

While she was in junior high school World War II was underway and her father was drafted into the military. He was stationed in San Diego, California and Ann and her mother moved west to be near him. Living in a big city was an eye-opening experience for Ann. For one thing, in her school there were students of many different races. Back in Texas the schools were still segregated—black children went to one school and white children went to another.

"Unless you have lived under it, the actual feeling of segregation is hard to grasp." Ann said. "For instance, in Texas, black people were allowed to buy goods in department stores but they were not allowed to try them on; black women could buy hats but they couldn't put them on their heads. . . . There were water fountains with signs that said *White* and *Colored* over them and bathrooms were segregated. If you were black and you were traveling, you'd better pack a lunch, because you couldn't stop in a restaurant and order food. There were no hotels or motels in which you could stay."[6]

After going to California and meeting other students who were African-American and Italian and Greek and Hispanic, Ann began to understand the injustices of racial prejudice. She saw firsthand how racism "stemmed from ignorance, unfamiliarity, and a need to feel superior at the expense of others. It's an unthinking, unreasoned emotional reaction: 'I must be okay because there is another whole group of people that I consider inferior to me.' Prejudice," she said, "is such a strange and pathetic form of elevating oneself."[7]

When the war ended her father was discharged from the army, and the family returned to Texas. Her parents decided to live in Waco, where Ann could attend a good school. "I wasn't much of a student," she admitted. "Anything I was interested in I could do pretty well, but anything that didn't catch my fancy I simply let go."[8] One of the things Ann was good at was debating. In fact, she was so good that she was picked to represent Texas at Girls Nation, an annual gathering of students from the fifty states. Meeting in Washington, D.C., they set up a mock government.

During high school Ann met her future husband, David Richards. He was dark and handsome and more sophisticated than many of the other boys at school, having read more books and visited more places. In 1953 they were married, when Ann was nineteen and in her junior year at Baylor University.

After graduating from college with a degree in speech and government, she moved to Austin to be with David, who had been accepted at the University of Texas Law School. For a couple of years she taught social studies to seventh and ninth graders. But when she gave birth to their first child, Cecile, she quit work and settled down to do what women of her generation were taught to do—be a good wife and a good mother. Later she gave birth to their first son, Dan.

When David was offered a job with the Civil Rights Commission, the family moved to Washington, D.C.. Ann immediately fell in love with our nation's capital. "I would head straight for the Senate," she recalled. "I'd sit there in the gallery and listen to the debate."[9]

David quickly grew frustrated with his job, and after only one year they returned to Dallas. But Ann, who was pregnant with their second son, Clark, had gotten her first real taste of national politics and wanted more. She formed the North Dallas Democratic Women's Organization. As president she linked all the Democratic clubs in Dallas County and then served as the president of that group. She also helped form the Dallas Committee for Peaceful Integration to try to help bring about a quick and peaceful end to segregation in schools.

In 1969 the family moved to Austin, and their new home became the hub of local Democratic Party activities. Ann recalled, "I was running a household, catering the local Democratic Party, being everything to everybody. I had a wonderful time, but there were moments when I felt that there was probably something more to life and I just didn't know what it was."[10] A few years later, after giving birth to her fourth child, Ellen, she would find out.

In 1971 she got a telephone call from a friend who wanted her to meet Sarah Weddington. Weddington was the twenty-five-year-old lawyer who had argued one of the most important and influential cases ever brought before the Supreme Court—*Roe v. Wade*. Her victory legalized abortion in the United States. Now she wanted to run for the Texas legislature. Ann recalled that Weddington was the first "out-and-out feminist" she had ever met.[11]

After helping her win the election, Ann started holding workshops and networking with women who were interested in politics. In 1974 she helped another woman candidate,

Wilhemina Delco, become the first African-American ever elected to the legislature from Travis County.

A year later a group of Democrats asked David to run for the post of county commissioner. (County commissioners are the executives who oversee the county courthouses. They also establish budget and tax rates for the county and build and maintain jails, roads, and bridges.) When David turned them down, they asked Ann if she would consider running.

"I really thought it was pretty far out to think that a woman could run for county commissioner," she said. "It's perceived as a truck-driving, front-end-loader operation, taking care of the roads."[12] But David urged her to give it a try and she accepted.

Right away Ann started campaigning door-to-door. "After each house I visited, I noted something personal . . . and I'd jot it down. . . . I would write on these postcards, 'Your kids have a wonderful tree house,' or 'You have a great brass door knocker.' Those cards stacked up, and we mailed them all at once the week before the election. That's the way you win elections."[13]

She was right—she won.

As commissioner Ann hired as many minorities and women as possible. She worked hard instituting important projects and oversaw the building of a beautiful bridge across the Colorado River and the establishment of the state's first juvenile probation system for young lawbreakers. She also developed new programs for many traditionally overlooked members of society, including hearing-impaired citizens, abused children, as well as parents of children with mental retardation.

In 1977 she joined 20,000 other women in Houston for the National Women's Conference. There, she made a stirring speech about the importance of the Equal Rights Amendment, a two-sentence amendment to the Constitution that would have guaranteed that all women have rights equal to those of men. Her speech was so impressive she was invited to be on President Jimmy Carter's Advisory Committee on Women.

During these years Ann had developed a drinking problem. Her friends and family grew more and more concerned until finally they helped her enroll in a program for alcoholics. When she finished the program she separated from David, and in 1984 they were divorced, after thirty years of marriage. For the first time in her life Ann was living alone. Initially she felt lonely, but it wouldn't be long before her life was filled with excitement and activity.

Her friends and colleagues encouraged her to run for state treasurer. The job appealed to Ann, but ever a realist, she recognized that fund-raising would be the biggest problem. She offered them a challenge: if they could raise $200,000 by sundown, she would do it. They did.

"No woman had won statewide office in fifty years, and I was hell-bent on breaking that string," Ann declared. " I campaigned all over the state, hit all of the big cities and a lot of the small towns."[14] With her elegant suits, her wit, and her charm, she was an appealing candidate. She ended up winning with 61.4 percent of the vote.

When she took office she was stunned by what she found. There were shoe boxes of checks lying around. All transactions were done with old-time adding machines. Instantly she started whipping the office into shape, modernizing all of its operations. After only two terms she had made $2 billion revenue for Texas—more money than all the other treasuries in the history of the state combined!

Her reputation as a smart, hardworking politician and as an effective, eloquent orator was spreading beyond Texas. In 1984 she was invited by Walter Mondale, the Democratic Party's presidential nominee, to join thirty other women to discuss whom he should pick as his vice-presidential running mate. By the time Ann left the meeting, she was convinced Mondale would nominate a woman—and he did: Geraldine Ferraro.

A short while later Ann Richards was asked to give the keynote address at the 1988 National Democratic Convention. This was a high honor reserved for the party's best speakers. Ann wanted to live up to everyone's expectations. Anxiously she set to work preparing a speech. She hired the best writers she could find (including Lily Tomlin's writer, Jane Wagner). The morning of the convention she was still adding the finishing touches to her speech.

Dressed in a blue suit and with a halo of white hair, she addressed the delegates, "Twelve years ago Barbara Jordan, another Texas woman, made the keynote address to this convention. . . . And two women in 160 years is about par for the course."[15] She then charged that George Bush, the wealthy Republican presidential candidate, had been born with a silver foot in his mouth. The room erupted in delighted laughter.

Some viewers, however, were outraged by her joke, and the Texas newspapers were deluged by indignant citizens complaining that she had embarrassed their state in front of the nation. Still, Ann Richards was hailed by many as a new rising star in the Democratic Party.

Inspired by her success, she set her sights on becoming governor. Right from the start she knew it wouldn't be easy. For one thing, Texas had grown increasingly Republican and conservative. Also, state politics had a tendency to turn nasty. She couldn't expect to become governor without taking hard punches and raising a lot of money.

But she also knew she had a number of things working for her. She had put together impressive records as both commissioner and treasurer. Further, she could count on tremendous grassroots support, especially from women. In fact, as soon as she announced her decision to run for governor, money began pouring in from all over. One of the biggest contributors was EMILY's List (EMILY stands for Early Money Is Like Yeast: It makes the dough rise. It is a group that funds pro-choice women candidates.)

Her challengers in the Democratic primary were the moderate incumbent Governor Mark White and the liberal Attorney General Jim Mattox. Ann started out strong. She crisscrossed Texas, giving campaign speeches and meeting with voters. Her son Dan went along to help and give her support. The mother and son team spent five to six days on the road, with as many as five stops a day, for nine months. Things were looking good in the polls. But then Mattox started mudslinging, claiming that Ann had used drugs.

In the first televised debate he asked her point blank. She responded that she had taken no mind-altering chemicals for ten years, since she entered the alcohol treatment program. It was an evasive answer. Her opponents jumped all over her. Reporters soon joined in. "Answer the question!" they clamored.

But Ann Richards dug her heels in, insisting, "I think we are sending a very sad message to a lot of people who think that if they seek treatment they will forever bear the stigma of their addiction."[16]

Her ratings in the polls plummeted. But she fought back, turning the spotlight away from herself and onto her opponents. She said, "Voters should be more concerned with how Mr. White became wealthy while serving as governor and . . . Mr. Mattox's acceptance of large, questionable contributions."[17] Both men, she announced, were guilty of taking large contributions while working as public servants, and thus abusing the voters' trust.

Her attack was successful. She defeated Mattox by about 2 percent of the vote. White finished third. Still, the toughest race was ahead. She had to face the Republican nominee, Clayton Williams, a multimillionaire who had fashioned himself in the mold of the roughriding cowboy of the Wild West.

He was a "grinning, jug-eared, guitar-playing, high-energy guy in chaps" who had decided he wanted to be governor and had $21 million to spend on doing just that.[18] His platform was simple: "We stand for God and our country, and our own basic values of a day's work for a day's pay, for honesty and integrity and the Boy Scouts!"[19]

He had won the Republican primary easily and come out virtually unscathed. In contrast, Ann was battle weary and still dogged by the drug question. Nevertheless, she put together a series of effective ads designed around the theme of "Meet Clayton Williams." They accused him of being a poor businessman deeply in debt. Williams fired back. He produced his own ads, which showed him galloping across the screen on his white stallion in a ten-gallon hat—the voters' Lone Ranger.

Luckily for Ann, however, the cowboy ended up shooting himself in the foot. Toward the end of the campaign he began making a series of blunders. First, he told reporters a joke in very poor taste about rape that outraged women, including Republican women, who ended up throwing their support behind Ann.

Then, just days before the election, he revealed that he had paid no income taxes in 1986 because, he said, it had been a bad year. But his worst misstep occurred when he was shown on television refusing to shake Ann's extended hand. This single incident destroyed his reputation as the well-mannered Lone Ranger, the ultimate Texas gentleman. Ann Richards won the hotly contested election.

As soon as she moved into office, she went to work "with more swagger than Texans had seen from their governor in decades."[20] Vowing that the government would no longer be filled with white men but would reflect Texas's diverse population, she selected minorities to fill more than 50 percent of the state's four hundred appointed offices. Nearly half of all her appointees were female. During her second week in office, she stormed into two state agencies that she found to be especially poorly run and ordered resignations.

Working long hours, Ann still found "the energy to paint poor people's houses, yell like a lunatic at Lady Longhorns [women's] basketball games, and sneak off to movies every weekend."[21]

By the end of her term U.S. *News & World Report* declared that she had been a successful governor: "Statistically crime [was] down, although nobody seemed to believe it. . . . The Texas economy [was] brisk again, almost booming. Oil [was] back bubbling . . . Even education [was] getting higher marks."[22]

Nevertheless, her standing in the polls was only mediocre. This could be attributed, at least in part, to a mood sweeping the United States that was antigovernment, anti-incumbent, and increasingly conservative. Although Ann was one of the most respected and best-known governors in the country, she was finding that this didn't necessarily guarantee reelection in 1994. Some pundits also noted that "the personality and the bold brassy rhetoric [speech] that have won her so much national stardom have really grated on a lot of Republicans."[23] For every joke she made that tickled a Democratic funny bone, she made a number of Republican enemies. This election was their chance to go after her. Her opponent was George H. W. Bush, the son of the former president. He was a young, earnest, conservative businessman.

During the campaign Ann revealed for the first time a weariness with politics. She was often cranky and seemed unduly frustrated. Many observers concluded that "the problem for Ann Richards is not so much Bush as it is herself."[24]

On election day she watched the numbers coming in. By midafternoon it was clear that she had lost. She ended up receiving 47 percent of the vote in comparison to Bush's 53 percent. When she got up in front of her saddened supporters, she reminded them, "It is not the end of the world. It is the end of a campaign."[25]

She was already looking forward to the future. "It was a wonderful four years [serving as governor]," she said. "But I'm very excited about the possibilities of doing new things and learning new things. . . . If you're always confronting new situations, new problems to solve, then life's always going to be fun and interesting."[26]

TEN

※

CHRISTINE
TODD WHITMAN

Christine Todd Whitman shocked almost everyone with her campaign promise to slash taxes substantially.

"It can't be done," many political observers charged.

As the first woman governor of New Jersey, she proved them wrong. Socially moderate, economically conservative, she was soon hailed as one of the most promising new stars of the Republican Party. Other GOP (Republican) candidates, trying to ride the coattails of her success, began calling themselves "Christine Whitman Republicans."

Within a few short years the likable, attractive governor had risen from relative obscurity to burst onto the national scene. It wasn't easy. She said, "My sister, who is twelve years older than I, was brought up in a world where women were secretaries or supported by husbands. I wasn't. I don't think a woman could have run for governor ten years ago. It was tough enough today."[1]

※

Born in 1947, the youngest of four children, Christine "Christie" Todd grew up in a family involved in Republican Party politics. Both of her parents were influential members of the moderate wing of the GOP. Christie recalled, "They had a strong partnership, and the conversation was always equal."[2]

Christie's father, Webster B. Todd, had served as an advisor to President Dwight Eisenhower and as chairman of the New Jersey Republican Party. A multimillionaire contractor, he built two of New York City's most famous tourist attractions-Radio City Music Hall and Rockefeller Center.

Christie's mother, Eleanor Schley Todd, was nicknamed the "Hurricane" because of her energy and the vehemence with which she expressed her strongly held opinions. A brilliant woman, she became the president of the New Jersey Federation of Republican Women and served as a delegate to Republican National Conventions.

In the mid-1950s, a headline of the *Newark Evening News* read: "Is New Jersey Ready for a Woman Governor?" The article concluded that it was not, but if it had been, the Hurricane would have been the perfect candidate.[3]

Christie grew up on a beautiful two-hundred-acre farmstead known as Pontefract, in exclusive Hunterdon County, New Jersey. The big white house, built in the 1700s, was surrounded by fields of hay and pens for the pigs, cows, sheep, and chickens. Pontefract was steeped in aristocratic gentility—next to the barn there was a swimming pool; not far from where the cows grazed there was a tennis court.

Often the peace and quiet of Pontefract would be shattered with the crack of Christie's gun as she practiced skeet shooting. A tomboy, she also loved playing basketball and riding horses.

During high school Christie dreamed about going into politics. It wasn't the power or the prestige of politics that appealed to her, but rather the chance to serve her community.

"There was certainly a feeling in our family that we had been very lucky," she said, "and you gave back."[4] This belief in giving back and helping others would become one of the cornerstones of her life.

After graduating from the exclusive Chapin High School in 1964, Christie went on to Wheaton College, in Massachusetts. She decided to major in international government after discovering that she knew more about local and state government than many of her professors did!

She had already worked on a number of presidential campaigns by this time, having started when she was ten years old by selling cups of lemonade at rallies when President Eisenhower ran for reelection. None of her previous experiences prepared her, however, for the exhilaration she felt when, at the age of twenty-one, she joined the New Jersey motorcade of presidential-hopeful Nelson Rockefeller, the governor of New York. Christie was thrilled to see the crowds gathering on the sidewalks.

"You'd see women come out of the beauty shop with their hair in curlers," she said. "Men come out of the barbershop with shaving cream on half their face. There weren't many politicians who inspired that kind of feeling."[5] Little did she know that one day people would be rushing out of shops to see her!

After college she decided to move to Washington, D.C., to be at the hub of the Republican Party's operations. She worked first at the Office of Economic Opportunity and later proposed an independent research project to the Republican National Committee. She wanted to study why many African-Americans and young people were not supporting the GOP.

She recalled her experience surveying a Chicago gang called the Black Disciples: "The meeting was in a long narrow room. We were at the far end, away from the door, and the Disciples all came in wearing their stocking caps and stood between us and the door."[6] The gang members tested the mettle of the rich white Republican young woman by shouting every swear word they could think of. "But I had grown up around two older brothers and a farmer," Christie said. "So there wasn't much they could describe that I hadn't heard before."[7]

When she finished the research report Christie decided to take an office job with the Peace Corps. In her free time she often played tennis with John Whitman. Handsome, wealthy, and bright, he was the son of a judge and the grandson of a governor. Except as someone to play tennis with, Christie admitted, "We didn't like each other at all."[8] Nevertheless, in 1973 she decided that since he was a good dancer she would invite him to be her date at President Nixon's second inaugural ball. Something clicked between them that night, and shortly afterward she moved to New York City to be near John.

Christie knew as soon as she arrived there that she "wanted to do something that was needed."[9] She found a job teaching English as a second language and math in a rough neighborhood of Spanish Harlem. John Whitman worked in a very different environment—he was an investment banker. A year later they were married.

After spending a couple of years in England, the young couple moved to New Jersey. Christie became pregnant with their daughter, Kate, and a year later with their son, Taylor. Although she was busy raising the children, she still found time to be involved in politics.

One of the issues she felt strongest about was the preservation of abortion rights. Christie wanted to make certain that her party represented socially moderate people like herself as well as the more conservative supporters of the right-to-life movement. So she helped found the Republicans for (Reproductive) Choice. She also became president of the Community Foundation of New Jersey, an organization that established homeless shelters and parks in impoverished neighborhoods.

In 1981 she received a telephone call from the Republican county chairman. He wanted to know if she would be interested in running for freeholder (a county supervisor in New Jersey).

"I grabbed it," Christie said.[10]

Cool under pressure, with a quick smile and a deep reserve of self-confidence, she soon became the head of the county freeholders. For the next five years she never shied away from tackling controversial issues, including the placement of a landfill, a halfway house for alcoholic teenagers, and a homeless shelter.

Then the governor called. He had lived near Pontefract and had been recruited into politics by Christie's father. Now he wanted to know if she would join his cabinet as the president of the Board of Public Utilities. She accepted. It wasn't a glamorous job. She was responsible for overseeing garbage collection and setting the rates for electricity, sewers, and water. Still, she worked hard, and the governor said, "Most of my cabinet members would come into my office and tell me the problem. Christie Whitman would come in and tell me the solution."[11]

In 1990 Christie decided to make the leap into statewide politics. She announced that she would challenge Bill Bradley, the state's popular, two-term senator. She knew she had little chance of winning. But she figured the race would give her some name recognition and campaign experience that could be used to run for another office in the future.

At first the wealthy, attractive mother of two was seen as nothing more than the GOP's "sacrificial lamb" being sent to electoral slaughter.[12] She had trouble raising money and received only $1 million in contributions compared to Bradley's $12 million. In the last week before the election, the Republican National Senatorial Committee became convinced that she couldn't win and withdrew its pledge to give her campaign $250,000.[13]

Without enough money to pay for television ads, Christie had trouble connecting with the voters. Ten weeks before the election, 75 percent of people polled did not know who she was.[14] She later joked, "It was like swimming uphill against the flood. [Bradley] was so well financed, and everything he said made the papers. I was lucky if I made the obits [obituary columns]."[15]. Still, in the televised debates she made a strong impression. She was articulate, poised, and personable. Tall and elegant, she came across as someone who, although wealthy and privileged, still passionately cared about people's problems and wanted to do something to help solve them.

On election night Christie, John, and their children watched with amazement as the returns came in. She was neck-and-neck with Bradley. By the end of the night, reporters and GOP chieftains were shaking their heads in disbelief. The "sacrificial lamb" had come within three percentage points of sending Bradley into retirement!

Invigorated by this race, Christie set her sights on becoming governor. Her husband acknowledged it was "an enormous reach, but one worth going for."[16] To become better known, Christie secured her own radio show and newspaper column. Then she helped found an organization to raise money for Republican candidates called the Committee for an Affordable New Jersey, a political action committee. For the next year and a half, Christie served as the chairperson of the committee. This allowed her to travel across the state and meet with Republican leaders and their wealthy supporters.

In 1993 she won the Republican primary election for governor. She would be challenging the Democratic incumbent, James Florio, in a race that became one of the most watched of the year.

The main theme of the election resonated in numerous states: what to do about taxes. Florio had initially promised not to raise taxes and later pushed through a $2.8 billion tax increase. Citizens were outraged. When he tried to include toilet paper as a taxable item, the people of New Jersey began plastering the backs of their cars with bumper stickers that read, Flush Florio.[17]

During his campaign Florio asserted that his tax increase had been necessary. Without it, he claimed that he would have been forced to slash public services, including funding for the police and schools. According to his campaign manager, Florio's candidacy demonstrated that "good leaders need to make tough decisions and [Florio will] show that you can be decisive and still win re-election."[18] Many governors facing similarly tough decisions about whether or not to raise taxes were watching to see how Florio would fare in the election.

Christie attacked her opponent for raising taxes but at first did not go so far as to call for a tax cut. Initially she was worried that doing so might bankrupt a state that was already facing large deficits. However, as her campaign lagged and she dropped farther and farther behind in the polls, she knew she needed something to jump-start her candidacy. She decided to hire financial consultants to see if they could find a way to make a tax cut possible. On Tuesday, September 21, 1993, she threw the long bomb. She announced that if elected governor, she would cut income taxes by 30 percent in three years. Her proposal was more extensive than anything anyone had imagined.

Immediately the press challenged her. How are you going to pay for the cuts? the reporters wanted to know.

She promised to find savings by cutting the cost of government. Among other things, she would slash "unnecessary overhead" and cut back on "professional services."[19] She said that one example of government waste was the "tens of thousands of dollars [that] are spent by the Department of Corrections to buy Adidas sneakers for prisoners. Those are the kinds of things we can cut."[20]

It turned out that prisoners actually were given cheap, brandless shoes, and her critics charged that her accounting was full of mistakes and exaggerations. One incredulous reporter called her tax-cut proposal "irresponsible"; another called it "an intentional fraud perpetrated by a desperate candidate."[21] Florio claimed she was in "Fantasyland."[22] But the battle lines had been drawn. The choice for voters was clear: a tax raiser or a tax slasher.

Still behind in the polls, Christie decided to cross the state on a bus tour. She wanted to meet one-on-one with voters, to use her intelligence and charisma to get her message across. "Every day on the road she became stronger and stronger," a supporter said. "The crowds built, the enthusiasm bubbled up—men cheering, women rushing out of beauty parlors with curlers in their hair."[23] She was becoming as inspirational a candidate as Rockefeller had been!

By election night the polls were showing Florio retaining a small lead. The media was predicting that he would win. But at half past midnight, Christie Whitman stood in front of a crowd of her supporters and with a huge grin shouted, "We did it!"[24] She had pulled from behind to become New Jersey's first woman governor.

Only two days after the election she was engulfed in a scandal. At a breakfast meeting with reporters, her campaign manager, Ed Rollins, boasted that black ministers had been paid a half million dollars to keep them from voicing their support of Florio to church members. If true, such an illegal act would have helped suppress the overwhelmingly Democratic black vote. The public was shocked. Had Whitman bought the election?

"It's a flat-out lie." she stated. "I find this whole thing . . . degrading to the voters of New Jersey, to the African-American community, and, frankly, to me."[25] She promised that if Rollins had done anything illegal, she would step down and call for a new election. Meeting with prominent black leaders

Jesse Jackson and Al Sharpton, she appeared genuinely outraged. In a statement to the United States district court in New Jersey, Rollins swore that he had lied.

After these first tumultuous days Whitman soon hit her stride as governor. She embarked on an ambitious strategy to try to help industries in New Jersey. For a long time the state had been in a recession and many companies were laying off workers.

When she and her staff started telephoning business executives to offer aid to them, many were surprised. One businessman said, "Here's the government calling me and asking if they could help. . . . Now we're considering putting more manufacturing operations here, which I know we wouldn't have considered before."[26]

Also, during her first year, Whitman surprised skeptics by cutting income taxes by 15 percent. Her critics immediately charged that to bring the budget under control she had to use "some fiscal sleight of hand."[27] One of her most controversial moves was to withhold $6 billion in contributions to the state pension fund (money paid to retired state highway and transportation workers). In doing so, she broke a campaign promise to avoid using "one-shot" revenue sources—money, such as that from the pension fund, which is available only once and doesn't help to solve long-term budgeting problems.[28]

Overall, however, Whitman received praise from the vast majority of citizens who were impressed by her bold tax cuts. Her approval rating rose to 52 percent, higher than that of her three predecessors at the same stage of their terms.[29] Voters also liked her honesty. "She won't not answer a question, even if the answer is going to make some people mad," said her chief of staff. "We say, 'Hold your tongue,' but she doesn't know how."[30]

The state troopers assigned to guard the new governor also discovered that she was hard to control. Christie kept sneaking out of her office and taking long walks by herself. Finally the frustrated troopers attached cowbells to her office door. When the bells jangled they knew that Christie was trying to disappear. Once, on a business trip, she managed to escape unnoticed from the hotel and went to a restaurant by herself. She called the troopers from a pay phone and, barely able to hide her delight, said to them, "It's 11:00 P.M.—do you know where your governor is?"[31] When she wasn't trying to outwit them, she would often invite the troopers to play games of pickup basketball.

During her second year in office Christie announced that she would fulfill her most important campaign promise ahead of schedule. She was going to slash income taxes an additional 15 percent. Newt Gingrich, the Republican Speaker of the House, declared himself "in awe" of her cuts.[32]

Others pointed out that her economic program caused painful trade-offs. While she was bringing down income taxes, local property taxes were rising an average of 5.4 percent statewide to make up for the shortfall.[33] The mayor of Elizabeth, New Jersey, estimated that the average family in his town saved $51 through Whitman's income tax cuts but paid almost $300 more in property taxes.[34] To balance the budget, Whitman had to cut the amount of funding paid to the state's environmental-protection and transportation departments. Her critics charged that she was simply "postponing fiscal pain and . . . employing budget gimmickry."[35]

Still, as one observer noted, "[Whitman] has been blessed by a vibrant economy."[36] Her approval rating continued to be high, at times rising above 60 percent.[37] Eight out of ten corporate executives in New Jersey rated her performance favorably.[38]

Other GOP politicians began trying to capitalize on her popularity and success, proposing similar tax cuts and describing themselves as "Christie Whitman Republicans." They started telephoning her, asking her if she would come and campaign with them. Christie was happy to oblige, and she traveled from Rhode Island to California, giving speeches, making headlines, raising a total of $3.5 million for Republican candidates. Of the twenty-two candidates she helped, a remarkable eighteen were victorious!

Suddenly Christie Whitman was at the center of the national spotlight. As one GOP congressman said, Christie was "the epitome [embodiment] of what the new Republican Party is—visionary, upbeat and committed to reducing the size of government."[39]

In fact, she was so popular that she was picked by the party leaders to deliver the Republican response to President Bill Clinton's 1995 State of the Union Address. On January 31, 1995, she became the first woman and the first governor to give this high-profile speech. The president had spoken for a long eighty minutes, and she began her own speech with a joke: "I am not going to ask for equal time."[40]

Many feel that she is poised to move on to Washington, D.C., possibly as the first woman vice president. One report noted, "Many Republicans are ready to put her face on . . . a campaign poster for higher office."[41]

Christie shakes off such speculation. "That's silly," she said. "I want to do the best job I can for New Jersey."[42]

SOURCE NOTES

INTRODUCTION

1. Ronna Romney and Beppie Harrison, *Momentum: Women in American Politics Now* (New York: Crown Publishers, 1988), 159.
2. Jeane J. Kirkpatrick, *Political Woman* (New York: Basic Books, Inc.), 1974, 3.

ONE: ELIZABETH DOLE

1. "Bob Dole's Better Half," *The Economist* (January 30, 1988), 22.
2. Bob Dole and Elizabeth Dole, with Richard Norton Smith, *The Doles: Unlimited Partners* (New York: Simon and Schuster, 1988), 33.
3. Carolyn Mulford, *Elizabeth Dole: Public Servant* (Hillside N.J.,: Enslow, 1992), 29.
4. Mulford, *Public Servant*, 43.
5. Dole and Dole, *Unlimited Partners*, 65.
6. Ibid., 65.
7. Ibid., 7.
8. Ibid., 135.
9. Ibid., 136.
10. Ibid., 137.
11. Ibid., 143.
12. Ibid., 142.

13. James A. Miller, "Portrait: Elizabeth Dole," *Life* (July 1983), 24.

14. Dole and Dole, *Unlimited Partners*, 131.

15. Ibid., 150.

16. Ibid., 154.

17. Ibid., 163.

18. Ibid., 171.

19. Ibid., 187.

20. Ibid., 200.

21. Interview, "There's No Higher Mandate Than to Promote Safety," U.S. *News and World Report* (May 9, 1983), 50.

22. Miller, *Portrait*, 50.

23. "Robert and Elizabeth Dole: A Winning Ticket," *Ladies Home Journal* (February 1988), 84.

24. "Bob Dole's Better Half," 22.

25. Bill Hewitt and Linda Kramer, "Dole on a Roll," *People* (June 24, 1991), 88.

26. Ibid., 87-88.

27. "Robert and Elizabeth Dole," 84.

28. Jane Mayer, "Blind Trust," *The New Yorker* (January 22, 1996), 65.

29. Dole, *Unlimited Partners*, 153.

TWO: DIANNE FEINSTEIN

1. Jerry Roberts, *Never Let Them See You Cry* (San Francisco: Harper-Collins West, 1994), 16.

2. Ibid., 9.

3. Sidney Blumenthal, "A Woman of Independent Means," *The New Republic* (August 13, 1990), 24.

4. Roberts, *Never Let Them See You Cry*, 27.

5. Ibid., 29.

6. Ibid., 39.

7. Ibid., 51.

8. Ibid., 54.

9. Ibid., 60.

10. Ibid., 69-70.

11. Celia Morris, *Storming the Statehouse: Running for Governor with Ann Richards and Dianne Feinstein* (New York: Charles Scribner's Sons, 1992), 192.

12. Roberts, *Never Let Them See You Cry*, 134.

13. Blumenthal, "A Woman of Independent Means," 25.

14. Ibid., 194.

15. Ibid., 25.

16. Roberts, *Never Let Them See You Cry*, 262.

17. B. Drummond Ayers Jr. "Candidates Hedge Their Bets on an Immigration Measure," *New York Times* (October 25, 1994), 1.

18. R. W. Apple Jr. "Struggle for the Senate," *New York Times* (October 20, 1994), 1.

19. Roberts, *Never Let Them See You Cry*, 240.

20. Panel Discussion, "Seven Women Who Could Change Your Life," *McCall's* (August 1994), 104.

THREE: GERALDINE FERRARO

1. Geraldine A. Ferraro, *Changing History: Women, Power, and Politics* (Wakefield, Rhode Island: Moyer Bell, 1993), 3.

2. Ibid., viii.

3. Lee Michael Katz, *My Name Is Geraldine Ferraro: An Unauthorized Biography* (New York: Signet, 1984), 24.

4. Ibid., 39.

5. Ibid., 41.

6. Ibid., 53.

7. Ibid., 61.

8. Geraldine A. Ferraro, with Linda Bird Francke, *Ferraro: My Story* (New York: Bantam Books, 1985), 36.

9. Ibid., 36-37.

10. Rosemary Breslin and Joshua Hammer, *Gerry!: A Woman Making History* (New York: Pinnacle Books, 1984), 76.

11. Ferraro and Francke, *My Story*, 56.

12. Ibid., 43.

13. Katz, *My Name Is Geraldine Ferraro*, 125.

14. Ferraro and Francke, *My Story*, 110.

15. Ferraro, *Changing History*, 10.

16. Ferraro and Francke, *My Story*, 181.

17. Ibid., 207.

18. Ibid., 262.

19. Don Lawson, *Geraldine Ferraro: The Woman Who Changed American Politics* (New York: Julian Messner, 1985), 37.

20. Ibid., 36.

21. Ibid., 241.

22. Ibid., 250.

23. Ibid., 259.

24. Ibid., 260.

25. Ibid., 260.

26. Ibid., 268.

27. Ibid., 289.

28. Ibid., 308.

29. Barbara Gerbasi, "Not My Son," *McCall's* (February 1990), 48.

FOUR: RUTH BADER GINSBURG

1. Jack L. Roberts, *Ruth Bader Ginsburg: Supreme Court Justice* (Brookfield, Conn.: Millbrook Press, 1994), 19.

2. Christopher Henry, *Ruth Bader Ginsburg* (New York: Franklin Watts, 1994), 13.

3. Elaine Shannon, "Justice for Women," *Vogue* (October 1993), 472.

4. Roberts, *Ruth Bader Ginsburg*, 11.

5. Shannon, "Justice for Women," 472.

6. Roberts, *Ruth Bader Ginsburg*, 16.

7. Shannon, "Justice for Women," 473.

8. Ibid., 473.

9. Judith Graman, ed., 1994 *Current Biography Yearbook* (New York: H. W. Wilson, 1994), 214.

10. Shannon, "Justice for Women," 472.

11. Roberts, *Ruth Bader Ginsburg*, 25.

12. Shannon, "Justice for Women," 472.

13. Roberts, *Ruth Bader Ginsburg*, 34.

14. Shannon, "Justice for Women," 473.

15. Ibid., 473.

16. Roberts, *Ruth Bader Ginsburg*, 28.

17. Ibid., 29.

18. Ellen Sweet, "Shirley Hufstedler and The Supremes," *Ms.* (May 1980), 53.

19. Shannon, "Justice for Women," 472.

20. Steven V. Roberts, with Dorian Friedman and Ted Gest, "Two Lives of Ruth Bader Ginsburg," *U.S. News and World Report* (June 28, 1993), 26.

21. Editorial, "Wise Choice," *The New Republic* (July 5, 1993), 7.

22. Roberts, *Ruth Bader Ginsburg*, 37.

23. Bob Italia, *United States Supreme Court Library: Ruth Bader Ginsburg* (Minneapolis: Abdo and Daughters, 1994), 24.

24. Shannon, "Justice for Women," 473.

25. Editorial, "Wise Choice," 7.

26. Roberts, *Ruth Bader Ginsburg*, 37-38.

27. Italia, *United States Supreme Court Library*, 28.

28. Henry, *Ruth Bader Ginsburg*, introduction.

FIVE: BARBARA JORDAN

1. Brian Lanker, "I Dream a World," *National Geographic* (August 1989), 206.

2. Judith Graham, *Current Biography* (New York: H. W. Wilson, 1993), 290.

3. Barbara Jordan and Shelby Hearon, *Barbara Jordan: A Self-Portrait* (Garden City, N.Y.: Doubleday, 1979), 6.

4. Ibid., 7.

5. Karen Zauber, "Barbara Jordan: Making a Difference," NEA *Today* (December 1992), p.9.

6. Jordan and Hearon, *Barbara Jordan*, 63.

7. Ibid., 79.

8. Ibid., 93.

9. Ibid., 107.

10. Ibid., 111.

11. Ibid., 117.

12. Ibid., 133.

13. Ibid., 145.

14. Ibid., 148.

15. Ibid., 152.

16. Ibid., 159.

17. Ibid., 166.

18. Ibid., 183.

19. Graham, *Current Biography*, 292.

20. Ibid., 292.

21. Jordan and Hearon, *Barbara Jordan*, 202.

22. David Gates, et al., "Jordan Is Immune to the Political Bug," *Newsweek* (December 19, 1983), 17B.

23. Rose Blue and Corinne Naden, *Barbara Jordan: Politician* (New York: Chelsea House, 1992), 15.

24. Gates, "Jordan Is Immune," 17C.

25. Zauber, "Barbara Jordan, Making a Difference," 9.

26. Gates et al., "Jordan Is Immune," 17C.

27. Zauber, "Barbara Jordan, Making a Difference," 9.

28. Jordan and Hearon, *Barbara Jordan*, 268.

29. Sam Howe, "At Funeral Praise for Barbara Jordan," *New York Times* (January 21, 1996).

30. Ibid.

SIX: JEANE KIRKPATRICK

1. Allan Gerson, *The Kirkpatrick Mission: Diplomacy Without Apology, America at the United Nations, 1981-1985* (New York: Macmillan, 1991), 9.

2. Mary Schwartz, "Jeane Kirkpatrick: Our Macho U.N. Ambassador," *National Review* (January 21, 1983), 50.

3. Pat Harrison, *Jeane Kirkpatrick* (New York: Chelsea House 1991), 31.

4. Gerson, *The Kirkpatrick Mission*, xiii.

5. Harrison, *Jeane Kirkpatrick*, 41.

6. Schwartz, "Macho U.N. Ambassador," 50.

7. Cindy Adams, "A Very Candid Conversation with Jeane J. Kirkpatrick," *Ladies Home Journal* (May 1986), 177.

8. Schwartz, "Macho U.N. Ambassador," 50.

9. Jeane J. Kirkpatrick, *Political Woman* (New York: Basic Books, 1974), 3.

10. Charles Moritz, ed., *Current Biography* (New York: H. W. Wilson, 1981), 257.

11. Schwartz, "Macho U.N. Ambassador," 52.

12. Gerson, *The Kirkpatrick Mission*, XV.

13. Patricia J. Sethi, "'An Obligation to Serve': U.N. Ambassador Jeane Kirkpatrick Looks Back," *Newsweek* (January 14, 1985), 33.

14. Ann Tremblay, "Jeane Kirkpatrick," *Working Woman* (May 1983), 106.

15. Dorothy Rabinowitz, "Reagan's 'Heroine' at the U.N.," *New York* (July 20, 1981), 36.

16. "Sexism Is Alive," *Time* (December 31, 1984), 14.

17. Schwartz, "Macho U.N. Ambassador," 48.

18. David Reed, "Jeane Kirkpatrick: America's 'Undiplomatic' Ambassador," *Reader's Digest* (August 1982), 76.

19. Schwartz, "Macho U.N. Ambassador," 49.

20. Tremblay, "Jeane Kirkpatrick," 106.

21. Rabinowitz, Reagan's 'Heroine,'" 20.

22. Ibid., 39.

23. Schwartz, "Macho U.N. Ambassador,"52.

24. Harrison, *Jeane Kirkpatrick*, 89.

25. Ibid., 90.

26. Tremblay, "Jeane Kirkpatrick," 109.

27. Adams, "A Very Candid Conversation," 178.

28. Ibid., 179.

29. Kirkpatrick, *Political Woman*," 252.

SEVEN: PEGGY NOONAN

1. Peggy Noonan, *What I Saw at the Revolution: A Political Life in the Reagan Era* (New York: Random House, 1990), 68.

2. Ibid., 5.

3. Ibid., 69.

4. Ibid., 6.

5. Daniel R. Levine, ed., "My First Job: The Camp Counselor," *Reader's Digest* (February 1992), 98.

6. Ron Rosenbaum, "Who Puts the Words in the President's Mouth?" *Esquire* (December 1985), 246.

7. Noonan, *What I Saw at the Revolution*, 15.

8. Ibid., 14.

9. Charles Moritz, ed., *Current Biography Yearbook* (New York: H. W. Wilson, 1990), 475.

10. Ibid., 31.

11. Ibid., 32.

12. Ibid., 52.

13. Ibid., 75.

14. Rosenbaum, "Who Puts the Words in the President's Mouth?," 250.

15. Howard Fineman, "Memorable Lines: Noonan's Best Sound Bites," *Newsweek* (August 22, 1988), 17.

16. Rosenbaum, "Who Puts the Words in the President's Mouth?," 251.

17. Moritz, *Current Biography Yearbook*, 473.

18. Hugh Sidey, "Of Poets and Word Processors," *Time* (May 2, 1988), 32.

19. Noonan, *What I Saw at the Revolution*, 72.

20. Sheila Weller, "Queen of the Sound Bites," *Ms.* (December 1988), 85.

21. Fineman, "Memorable Lines," 17.

22. Moritz, *Current Biography Yearbook*, 476.

23. Noonan, *What I Saw at the Revolution*, 217.

24. Rosenbaum, "Who Puts the Words in the President's Mouth?," 250.

25. Ibid., 250.

26. Moritz, *Current Biography Yearbook*, 476.

27. Rosenbaum, "Who Puts the Words in the President's Mouth?," 250.

28. Ibid., 249.

29. Moritz, *Current Biography Yearbook*, 476.

30. Ken Gross and Margie Bonnet Sellinger, "The Great Communicator Might Have Been Less So without Peggy Noonan Writing His Lyrics," *People* (February 26, 1990), 84.

31. Noonan, *What I Saw at the Revolution*, 296.

32. Howard Fineman, "The Wordsmith Behind the Speech," *Newsweek* (August 22, 1988), 17.

33. Noonan, *What I Saw at the Revolution*, 311.

34. Ibid., 316.

35. Maureen Dowd, "High Noonan," *Vogue* (December 1989), 340.

36. Ibid., 341.

37. Editorial, "Peggy Noonan Grosses Out," *National Review* (November 10, 1989), 20.

38. Peggy Noonan, *Life, Liberty, and the Pursuit of Happiness* (New York: Random House, 1994), 93.

39. Ibid., 111.

40. Howard Rosenberg, "Peggy Noonan: GOP Sighted on PBS," *Los Angeles Times* (February 10, 1995).

41. Christine Reinhardt, "A Thousand Points to Write," *Working Woman* (November 1990), 169.

EIGHT: JANET RENO

1. Paul Anderson, *Janet Reno: Doing the Right Thing* (New York: John Wiley, 1994), 3.

2. Judith Graham, *Current Biography* (New York: H. W. Wilson, 1993), 486.

3. Nancy Gibbs, "Truth, Justice, and the Reno Way," *Time* (July 12, 1993), 23.

4. Graham, *Current Biography*, 486.

5. Anderson, *Janet Reno*, 31.

6. Ibid., 38.

7. Ibid., 62.

8. *Chicago Tribune* (Februrary 12, 1993), V1, as quoted in *Current Biography*.

9. Anderson, *Janet Reno*, 68.

10. Elaine Shannon, "The Unshakable Janet Reno," *Vogue* (August 1993), 262.

11. Anderson, *Janet Reno*, 81.

12. Ibid., 80.

13. Larry Rohter, "Tough 'Front-Line Warrior,'" *New York Times* (February 12, 1993), A22.

14. Anderson, *Janet Reno*, 12.

15. *Congressional Quarterly Almanac: 103rd Congress*, 1st Session, 1993, 306.

16. Laura Blumenfeld, "Janet Reno: Tower of Justice," *Cosmopolitan* (July 1993), 187.

17. Elaine Shannon, "Those Kids Are So Eager," *Time* (July 12, 1993), 24.

18. *Congressional Quarterly*, 304.

19. Jeffrey Rosen, "The Trials of Janet Reno," *Vanity Fair* (April 1994), 150.

20. Ibid., 171.

21. Shannon, "The Unshakable Janet Reno," 313.

22. Ibid., 260.

23. Gibbs, "Truth, Justice, and the Reno Way," 22-23.

NINE: ANN RICHARDS

1. Ann Richards, *Straight From the Heart: My Life in Politics and Other Places* (New York: Simon and Schuster, 1989), 24.

2. Ibid., 35.

3. Ibid., 39.

4. Al Reinert, "The Titan of Texas," *Vogue* (August 1991), 245.

5. Richards, *Straight From the Heart*, 51.

6. Ibid., 94.

7. Ibid., 57.

8. Ibid., 61.

9. Ibid., 102.

10. Ibid., 118.

11. Celia Morris, *Storming the Statehouse: Running for Governor With Ann Richards and Dianne Feinstein* (New York: Charles Scribner's Sons, 1992), 23.

12. Richards, *Straight From the Heart*, 153.

13. Ibid., 158.

14. Ibid., 220.

15. Ibid., 24.

16. Ibid., 75.

17. Ibid., 90.

18. Ibid., 106.

19. Ibid., 108.

20. Ibid., 111.

21. Ibid., 245.

22. Tom Callahan, "She Thinks They'll Keep Her," U.S. *News & World Report* (October 17, 1994), 36.

23. Alison Cook, "Lone Star," *New York Times Magazine* (February 7, 1993), 24.

24. Callahan, "She Thinks They'll Keep Her," 36.

25. Gail Collins, "The Unsinkable Meets the Unthinkable," *Working Woman* (March 1995), 53.

26. Ibid., 86.

TEN: CHRISTINE TODD WHITMAN

1. Eric Pooley, "The Liberation of Christine Whitman," *Vogue* (August 1994), 176.

2. Ibid., 172.

3. Ibid., 174.

4. John B. Judis, "Part I: The Closet Liberalism of Christine Todd Whitman," *The New Republic* (February 13, 1995, America Online, cited April, 28, 1995), 4.

5. Pooley, "The Liberation of Christine Whitman," 174.

6. Ibid., 174.

7. Judis, "The Closet Liberalism of Christine Todd Whitman," 5.

8. Pooley, "The Liberation of Christine Whitman," 176.

9. Judis, "The Closet Liberalism of Christine Todd Whitman," 5.

10. Pooley, "The Liberation of Christine Whitman," 174.

11. Ibid., 174.

12. Michael Aron, *Governor's Race: A TV Reporter's Chronicle of the* 1993 *Florio/Whitman Campaign* (New Brunswick: Rutgers University Press, 1994), 7.

13. Steve Fainaru, "Tax Cutting Has Whitman in Spotlight," *Boston Globe* (January 27, 1995), 6.

14. Judis, "The Closet Liberalism of Christine Todd Whitman," 7.

15. Pooley, "The Liberation of Christine Whitman," 176.

16. Ibid., 168.

17. Fainaru, "Tax Cutting Has Whitman in Spotlight," 6.

18. Robert J. Wagman, "New Jersey Governor's Race: National Implications or Local Politics?" *Newspaper Enterprise Association* (October 25, 1993, America Online, cited April 28, 1995), 2.

19. Aron, *Governor's Race*, 222.

20. Ibid., 245.

21. Ibid., 227.

22. Ibid., 225.

23. Pooley, "The Liberation of Christine Whitman," 176.

24. Aron, *Governor's Race*, 288.

25. Ibid., 296-297.

26. Jonathan Peterson, "Whitman's Gamble," *Los Angeles Times* (April 16, 1995), D1.

27. Howard Gleckman and Judy Dobrzynski, "The Ronald Reagan of New Jersey," *Business Week* (October 17, 1994), 42.

28. Pooley, "The Liberation of Christine Whitman," 176.

29. Gleckman, "The Ronald Reagan of New Jersey," 42.

30. Pooley, "The Liberation of Christine Whitman," 170.

31. Ibid., 168.

32. Carrol Bogert, "On the Cutting Edge," *Newsweek* (December 5, 1994), 28.

33. Peterson, "Whitman's Gamble," D6.

34. Bogert, "On the Cutting Edge," 28.

35. Fainaru, "Tax Cutting Has Whitman in Spotlight," 6.

36. Ibid., 6.

37. Melissa Healy, "GOP Answers Clinton with Call to 'Revolution of Ideas,'" *Los Angeles Times* (January 25, 1995), A8.

38. Peterson, "Whitman's Gamble," D6.

39. Healy, "GOP Answers Clinton," A8.

40. Christopher John Farley, "From New Jersey the Great Whitman Hope," *Time* (February 6, 1995), 26.

41. Steven V. Roberts, "A Poster Daughter for GOP Diversity," U.S. *News & World Report* (February 6, 1995), 10.

42. "Christine Todd Whitman," *People Weekly* (December 26, 1994), 88.

FURTHER READING

~

Anderson, Paul. *Janet Reno: Doing the Right Thing*. New York: John Wiley and Sons, 1994.

Aron, Michael. *Governor's Race: A TV Reporter's Chronicle of the 1993 Florio/Whitman Campaign*. New Brunswick, N.J.: Rutgers University Press, 1994.

Blue, Rose, and Corinne Naden. *Barbara Jordan: Politician*. New York: Chelsea House, 1992.

Booth, Alice Lynn. *Careers in Politics for the New Woman*. New York: Franklin Watts, 1978.

Breslin, Rosemary, and Joshua Hammer. *Gerry!: A Woman Making History*. New York: Pinnacle Books, 1984.

Dole, Bob, and Elizabeth Dole, with Richard Norton Smith. *The Doles: Unlimited Partners*. New York: Simon and Schuster, 1988.

Ferraro, Geraldine A. *Changing History: Women, Power, and Politics*. Wakefield, Rhode Island: Moyer Bell, 1993.

————, with Linda Bird Francke. *Ferraro: My Story*. New York: Bantam Books, 1985.

Harrison, Pat. *Jeane Kirkpatrick*. New York: Chelsea House, 1991.

Henry, Christopher. *Ruth Bader Ginsburg*. New York: Franklin Watts, 1994.

Italia, Bob. *United States Supreme Court Library: Ruth Bader Ginsburg*. Minneapolis: Abdo and Daughters, 1994.

123

Jordan, Barbara, and Shelby Hearon. *Barbara Jordan: A Self-Portrait.* Garden City, N.Y.: Doubleday, 1979.

Katz, Lee Michael. *My Name Is Geraldine Ferraro: An Unauthorized Biography.* New York: Signet, 1984.

————. *The Strategy of Deception: A Study in World-Wide Communist Tactics.* New York: Farrar, Straus and Giroux, 1963.

————. *Political Woman.* New York: Basic Books, 1974.

————. *The New Presidential Elite: Men and Women in National Politics.* New York: Russell Sage Foundation and the Twentieth-Century Fund, 1976.

Kirkpatrick, Jeane J. *Dictatorships and Double Standards: Rationalism and Reason in Politics.* New York: Simon and Schuster and the American Enterprise Institute for Public Policy Research, 1982.

————. *The Reagan Phenomenon: And Other Speeches on Foreign Policy.* Washington and London: American Enterprise Institute for Public Policy Research, 1983.

————. *The Reagan Doctrine and U.S. Foreign Policy.* Washington, D.C.: The Heritage Foundation, 1985.

————. *Life, Liberty, and the Pursuit of Happiness.* New York: Random House, 1994.

Lawson, Don. *Geraldine Ferraro: The Woman Who Changed American Politics.* New York: Julian Messner, 1985.

Mandel, Ruth B. *In the Running: The New Woman Candidate.* Boston: Beacon Press, 1983.

Morris, Celia. *Storming the Statehouse: Running for Governor with Ann Richards and Dianne Feinstein.* New York: Charles Scribner's Sons, 1992.

Mulford, Carolyn. *Elizabeth Dole: Public Servant.* Springfield, N.J.: Enslow Publishers, 1992.

Noonan, Peggy. *What I Saw at the Revolution: A Political Life in the Reagan Era.* New York: Random House, 1990.

Richards, Ann. *Straight From the Heart: My Life in Politics and Other Places.* New York: Simon and Schuster, 1989.

Roberts, Jack L. *Ruth Bader Ginsburg: Supreme Court Justice.* Brookfield, Conn.: Millbrook Press, 1994.

Roberts, Jerry. Never Let Them See You Cry. San Francisco: HarperCollins West, 1994.

Romney, Ronna, and Beppie Harrison. *Momentum: Women in American Politics Now*. New York: Crown Publishers, 1988.

Simon, Charnan. *Janet Reno: First Woman Attorney General*. Chicago: Children's Press, 1994.

Tolchin, Susan, and Martin Tolchin. *Clout: Womanpower and Politics*. New York: Coward, McCann, and Geoghegan, 1974

INDEX

⁓